COACHING THE FAST BREAK
BY THE EXPERTS

Edited by
Bob Murrey

USA
COACHES CLINICS

COACHES CHOICE™

MW01671472

© 2002 Coaches Choice. All rights reserved.

Printed in the United States.

No part of this book may be reproduced, stored in a retrieval system, or transmitted, in any form or by any means, electronic, mechanical, photocopying, recording, or otherwise, without the prior permission of Coaches Choice.

ISBN: 1-58518-336-9
Library of Congress Catalog Card Number: 2001095163

Cover photo courtesy of Won-Up Productions
Cover design: Rebecca Gold
Text design: Jennifer Bokelmann

Coaches Choice
P.O. Box 1828
Monterey, CA 93942
http://www.coacheschoiceweb.com

Additional information on either the USA Coaches Clinic schedule or the USA Coaches library can be obtained by either calling 1-800-COACH-13 or faxing 1-314-991-1929.

Throughout this book, the masculine shall be deemed to include the feminine and vice versa.

CONTENTS

Diagram Legend 4

Chapter 1: Fast Break—Huskie Style 5
Jane Albright-Dieterle–Northern Illinois (Women's)

Chapter 2: Transition Basketball 16
Joan Bonvicini–Arizona (Women's)

Chapter 3: Developing the Fast Break 25
Jim Harrick–Georgia

Chapter 4: The Transition Offense 34
Jim Jabir–Marquette (Women's)

Chapter 5: The Fast Break System 44
Muffet McGraw–Notre Dame (Women's)

Chapter 6: The Fast Break 55
Jim O'Brien–Dayton

Chapter 7: Fundamentals for the Fast Break 60
Johnny Orr–Iowa State

Chapter 8: Teaching the Fast Break 69
Tom Penders–Texas

Chapter 9: A Fast Break for All People 77
Dawson Pikey–Clayton HS (MO)

Chapter 10: Tiger Fast Break 90
Jo Ann Rutherford–Missouri (Women's)

Chapter 11: Developing the Fast Break 96
Paul Westhead–Golden State Warriors

Chapter 12: The Fast Break 101
Roy Williams–Kansas

DIAGRAM LEGEND

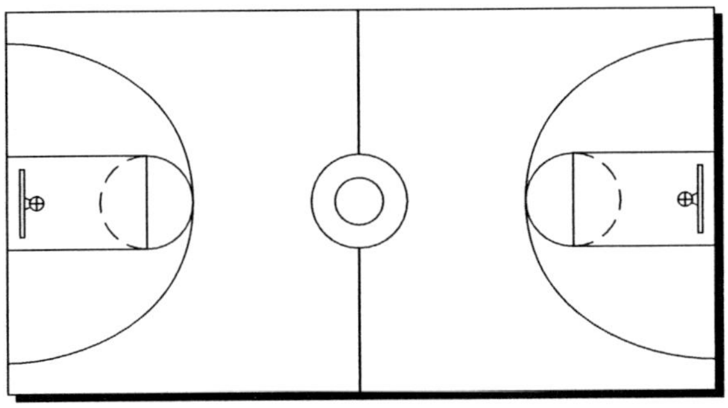

PLAYERS

(5) Centers

(3, 4) Forwards

(1, 2) Guards

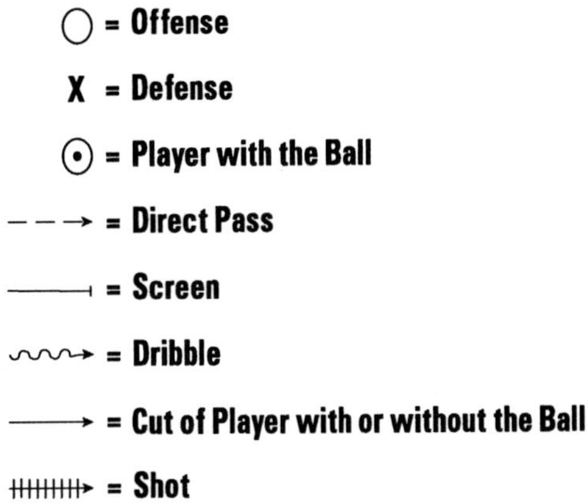

CHAPTER 1

FAST BREAK HUSKIE STYLE

Jane Albright-Dieterle

WHY FAST BREAK? The fast break takes a lot of emphasis. John Wooden is the person who said, "It's not what you teach, it's what you emphasize." You must work on this day in and day out.

- You must paint the Big Picture, fun, excitement, *many chances to score.* The fast break gives a lot of people many chances to score. Anything that will make the game fun will help you. At our level, I believe that is fun. At Northern Illinois, we created an identity with it. We led the nation in scoring this year, 94.5 points per game. We didn't start out the year saying that we had to score 90 points per game. It just started happening. If I had a high school team, I would really fast break; that would be the main thing I would do. Make your team think that the team has an identity with the break. It will take several years for this to happen.
- The fast break gets you *great shots.* We give our kids the freedom to make the wrong decision. We take some bad shots. If they know it was a bad shot, we don't yell at them. Because they are going to get caught up in the tempo, you must bite your tongue occasionally. You must teach what a good shot is. We were fifth in the nation in FGA, 51.5%. We teach with numbers; we are objective instead of subjective. The fast break will enable everyone to get a good shot situation.
- You can play this offense with *smaller numbers.* It is simple. I don't want your team to set up your defense. Your opponent can scout you and prepare for you. But they can't fully prepare for the fast break. I think you have a better opportunity of being successful if you can play 2-on-2, 3-on-3, instead of 5-on-5.
- The fast break forces your opponent to make *adjustments.* Our opponents were always expecting us to spurt. Even if they know you run, they are not drilled to get back. It's a form of pressure on your opponents. The mental aspect of the fast break is better than the X's and O's.
- The opponent must also make *adjustments on the boards.* If they know that you are going to run, they are scared of you getting a rebound, so they will have to adjust.

- The advantage in practice is that it is *FUN.* People love to practice the fast break. It is conditioning, but they don't mind it because they know that there is a reason for ding it. You can condition them both mentally and physically. You must give your kids freedom in this type of practice. You can't scream at them or they tense up.
- This system allows for *creativity.*
- It demands and encourages *tough defense.* We tell our kids, you play tough defense and we will go down and shoot the ball. That encourages them. Some people say that we are a great offensive team because of our defense. You can use offense as a reward. We tell our players that the best offense is a "best defense." If you run, people say that you don't play defense. My team gets mad about this. We just want a lot of possessions to score. We give up 70 points a game, but we don't hold the ball. You must teach that since we are shooting quickly, they will have the ball more times. You must show your team that they are a good defensive team. We talk about our opponents field goal percentage.
- The fast break gives you a *quicker shot* with less chance for a turnover. I saw a scouting report on us, and it said, "If they pass the ball more than twice, they are in their stall offense." That got me a little upset. But then I got to thinking that it was all right. If that's what we want to be, then O.K. The image might be that we don't play defense, but we do.

THE FAST BREAK

- It is an *attitude, a philosophy, and a concept.* It's not just X's and O's. You win when you understand the concepts. There are four concepts.
- You always look to *run first*; if it is not there, *then you adjust.* You must stop and have a half-court offense. We have about two such offenses and some special-situation offenses. We run a 1-2-2 pass and screen away much of the time, nothing complicated.
- You must *advance the ball quickly.*
- Your drills *must be up-tempo* with skills and movement. I changed all my passing drills. We never stand and pass. We move in every passing drill we do. We want to execute the skills very quickly. If you are going to run, you must execute these skills while you are moving and hit a moving target. Everything must be moving; you must be up-tempo. What happens in a game? Everything is quicker, and then the first thing you do is have a turnover.
- You can always *attack the defense.*

KEEP IT SIMPLE.

- *Fundamentals.* You must have a lot of fundamentals: rebounding, passing, fakes, shooting and ball handling. We have a real simple game. You would be surprised at the simplicity of our system. All factors considered, if you keep it simple, you will be more successful.

- You must *execute the skills at an up-tempo pace.* You must do it, and you must do it a lot of times.

FOUR PHASES FOR SUCCESSFUL BREAK

We break the fast break down into four phases. Everybody knows that at the end of the fast break you are going to score. So, your kids think that that's where the fast break is. But, you must emphasize all four phases of the break, and have breakdown drills for each of the phases.

- *The Rebound.* That's the best time to break. If your rebounder is working to make it happen, then you better tell the papers about it. You must keep these people happy, (i.e., talk about it the next day at practice).
- *The outlet,* the timing, and taking care of the ball. We run two guards interchangeably.
- *Lane recognition,* and speed without the ball. If my teammate has the ball, I should be faster without the ball. You need to tell these kids, you can't be behind the ball. You must emphasize that you must run wide in the lanes.
- *Scoring.* That's easy. If you can do the other three things, the scoring will take care of itself. I think that most players behave the way that you make them behave. I like it when the scorer points to the passer. Many people comment on how supportive they are of each other. But, you better believe that they don't feel that way every day. But even so, they are supportive, whether they feel like it or not. *Behavior definitely creates feelings.* I think that if you let the feelings create the behavior, you are in trouble.

CONCEPTS OF THE FAST BREAK

If you run a fast break, the pattern at the end is not what is going to make your break better than my break. It's the concepts. Your players must really know and truly understand these *seven concepts.* I must ask my players all the time, "What do I mean?" Do they really understand?

- *Attacking.* Always attack. We drill 11/1 all the time. Always attack with the ball, with a pass, with a drive.
- *Beware of numbers:* 3/2, 4/2. We want to attack when we have the advantage.
- *Spacing.* Very critical; you cannot bunch. Sometimes stop practice and say, "What are you doing right?" And then they recognize that they are spaced correctly.
- *Balance.* You must balance the floor horizontally and vertically.
- *Ball reversal.* We work had on our missed baskets. You can reverse the ball on the fast break because the defense goes right to the bucket on the ball side. So, reverse the ball and get it into the low post. It's not natural to reverse the ball. It must be taught.
- *Timing.* We are up-tempo, but sometimes you must hesitate long enough to make the proper moves, especially with ball reversal.

- *Up-tempo.* We yell it all the time. Are you going fast enough?

THE STRUCTURE OF THE BREAK

You must let your players know what you want, and you must be specific. If you don't do that and try to fast break, it will be nothing but chaos.

- *When to break.* There are four times you can break; after a rebound, after a made foul shot, after a made field goal, and after a defensive steal. We try to run after all four of these. You may want to limit your team to several of them. Breaking after a rebound or after a defensive steal is extremely important. You have a distinct advantage when you can score on an opponent's possession. This is a four-point turnaround—the two your opponent didn't get and the two you got. That's when you are going to win games. We chart that and know how many times we score on the opponent's possessions. We have "runs" in games because of doing this.
- Your team must *know who is going to do what.* We run a numbered break after a made basket. Do you want the "two" guard handling the ball? We want every person to have a role on the club, but every now and then we allow them to get out of their role, because it's a fun thing for them to do.

Discipline vs. junk. People will say that if you are a fast breaking team, you are unstructured. But as a coach, you must let your ego go within this entire thing. You must play within the structure of the system. They cannot shoot junk. And as a coach you must make decisions objectively, not subjectively. Did you ever ask you players, "How do you think you did tonight?" This is a subjective-type question. *Ask them to rate their performance on scale of 1 to 10.* That makes it more meaningful. If it is subjective, you can get away with anything. Make your questions more objective, use a 1-to-10 scale. Shooting is objective. A girl came in the office the other day and said, "I'll be taking a lot of 3-pointers next year, won't I?" I said, "We'll see. I'll decide that with numbers." We will have a number system. If you can hit a certain percentage from a spot, you will be allowed to shoot from there. You can teach them within a system that you can't shoot a certain shot until you hit a certain percentage. You as a coach have to make every situation objective.

Your players must be able to recognize the transition from the primary to the secondary break, balance passing, and running lanes. There must be some type of up-tempo effort to push the ball down and look for the numbers in the half-court game. They must know the difference. They have the primary break, the secondary break, and then they have the half-court offense.

DIAGRAM 1-1. PARTNER PASS

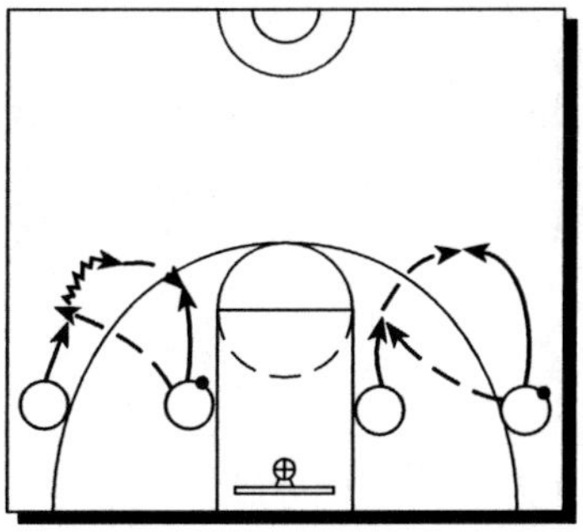

We run this full-court, at a slow speed initially with just a chest pass. To do it successfully, however, you must do it at a higher speed. This is boring, but great players do these well. We don't teach the baseball pass, but we let them throw it. The problem with a baseball pass is once you start to do it, you can't stop.

DIAGRAM 1-2.

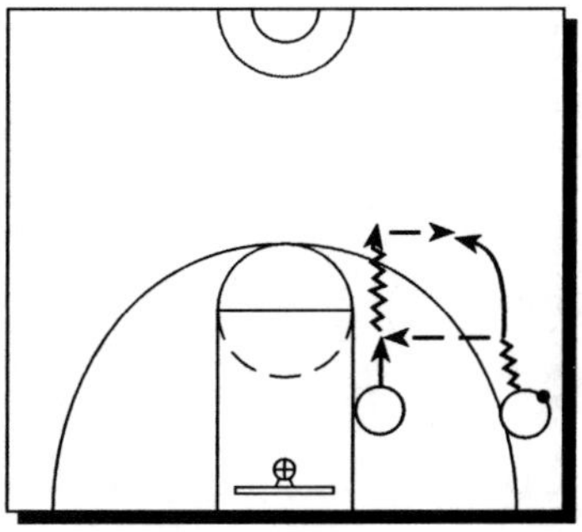

Then, we add a dribble. The person with the ball takes two dribbles, and the person who doesn't have the ball must get out ahead of the ball. If you aren't ahead of the ball, it is not a fast break. The ball handler is only to take two dribbles.

DIAGRAM 1-3.

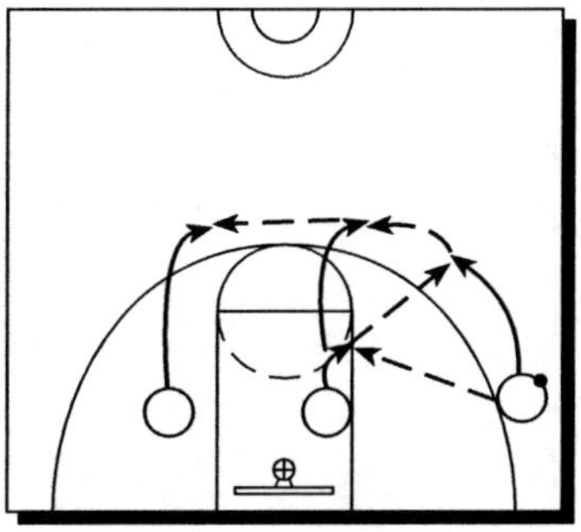

We then add a third person with 15 feet between players. We keep alternating sides with passes. Then a dribble is added, but only two dribbles. Again, two people should be ahead of the ball.

DIAGRAM 1-4.

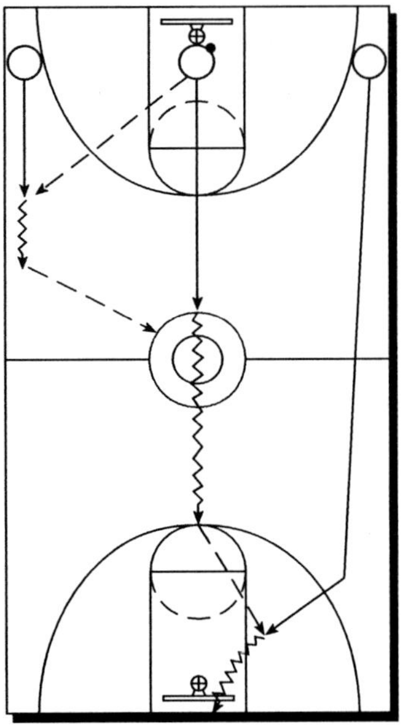

We then run it and score at the other end. You should be at the other end after two dribbles and three passes. Everyone must take a turn in the middle, go down and back, even the post people.

DIAGRAM 1-5.

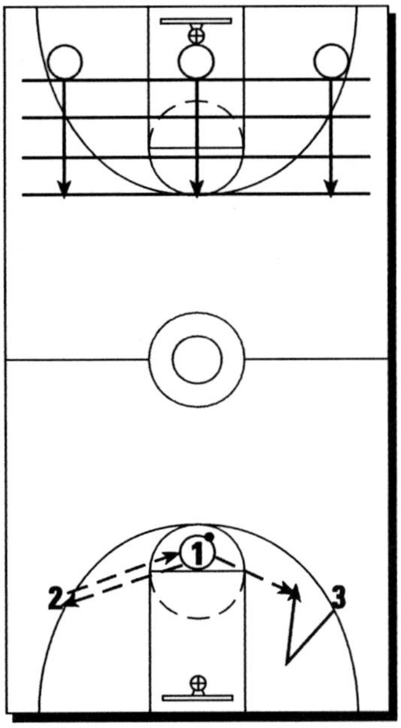

We add a different finish after awhile. 1 will pass to 2, 2 return passes to 1, 3 breaks in, and then comes back out for the shot. I'd like to say that I have always hated to run as punishment, and we seldom do it. But, we do get our running in by doing these drills. We let them stay on the floor if they hit. They only get one shot. We will say, "Up to 3." If they hit, they stay, and it is an upper for them.

DIAGRAM 1-6. BLOCKOUT AROUND THE BALL DRILL

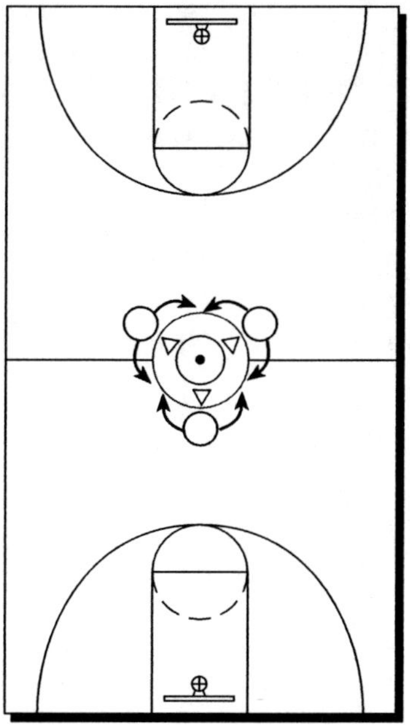

The defense makes a reverse pivot. This is a defensive drill; it has nothing to do with scoring.

DIAGRAM 1-7. WOODEN DRILL

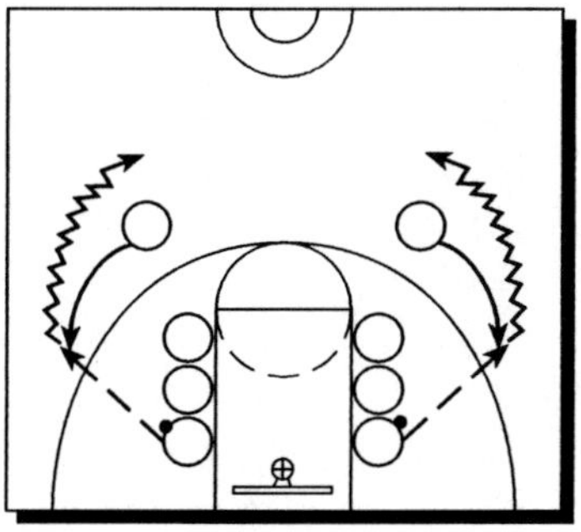

The first player in line puts the ball on the glass, misses on purpose, and then rebounds. That player should then blockout, pivot away from the defense, make the outlet pass, and start to run the lane. The outlet guard takes the ball to the middle of the court, to half-court. Everyone works in every position. The movement away from the defense is the key. You can put a defense on the outlet person.

DIAGRAM 1-8. THREE-PLAYER WEAVE

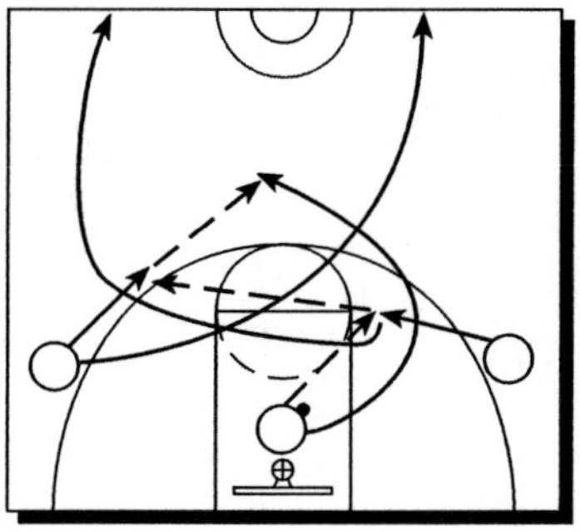

We call it the figure 8—pass and go behind the ball. Spacing is important; the emphasis is on no turnovers and scoring.

DIAGRAM 1-9. THREE-FAMILY FLY DRILL

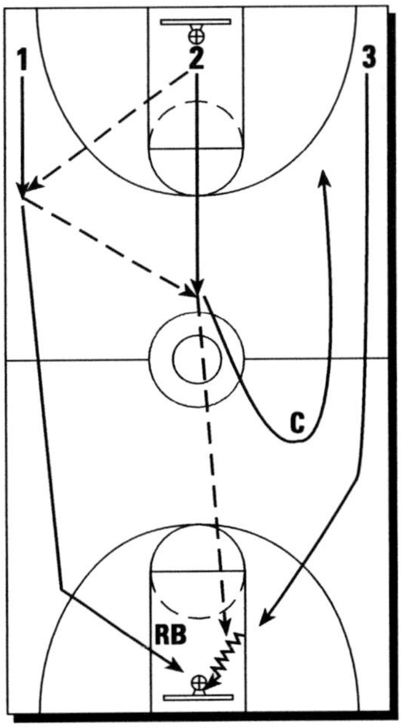

This is the baseball-pass drill. 2 takes the ball off the glass, turns away from the defense and makes an outlet pass to 1. 2 then goes down the middle. 3 is flying down the court to shoot a layup. After 2 makes the pass to 3, 2 circles around the coach. 2 should not dribble, but should throw the baseball pass. 1 will rebound.

DIAGRAM 1-10.

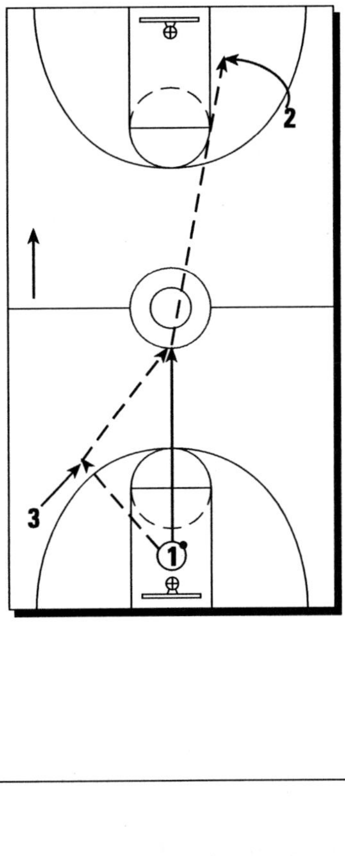

1 rebounds and passes back to 3 who has circled under the basket and is coming back in the other direction. 1 gets the ball back from 3 and makes a baseball pass to 2. No dribbling is allowed.

DIAGRAM 1-11.

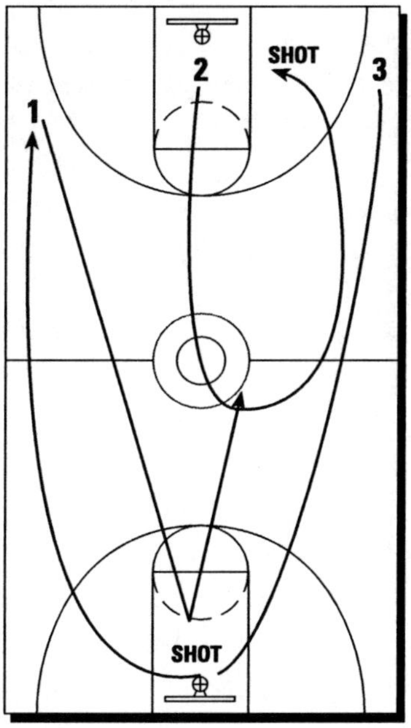

This is what the overall view looks like. Everyone gets in all three positions. Each group goes down and back. This is a great conditioning drill.

DIAGRAM 1-12. LAKER CONTINUITY DRILL

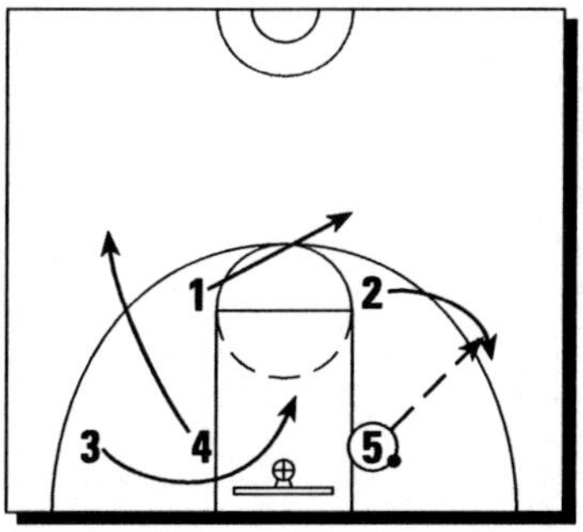

This is probably the most effective drill we do. 1 is the point guard; 2 is also a guard. 5 rebounds off the glass. 5 turns away from the defense and makes the outlet pass to 2. 1 comes across the lane because that is what we do in the game. On a miss, 1 and 2 are interchangeable. 4 runs the lane, and takes about four steps as hard as she can. 3 follows the shot.

DIAGRAM 1-13.

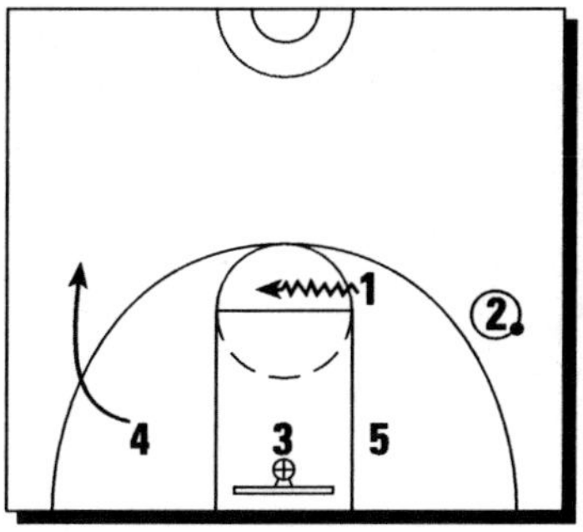

After 2 passes to 1, 1 dribbles across the lane.

DIAGRAM 1-14.

1 passes back to 2 who passes in to 5. 5 puts the ball on the glass over to 4 who rebounds. 3 fills the lane with four hard steps, and 5 follows the shot. 4 turns away from defense and passes to 1, who then passes to 2 who is now at the elbow.

DIAGRAM 1-15.

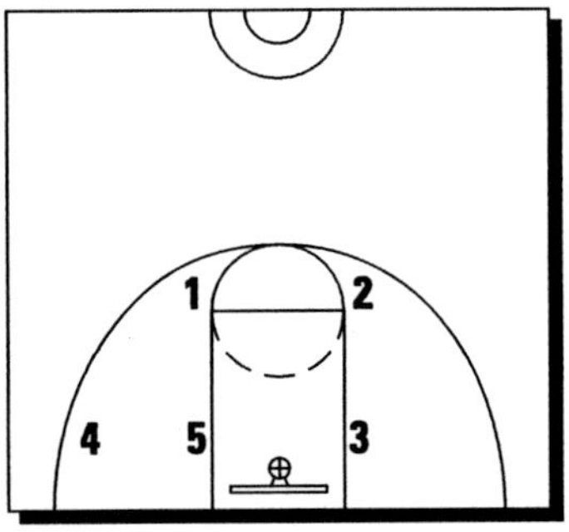

Now, the players are in the positions shown. You are shooting and following the shot. You should not try to hit the shot. If you don't rebound, you should run the lane for about four steps. 1 and 2 take the outlet pass and pass into the middle. You must keep them hustling back because you want the drill performed at a quick pace.

DIAGRAM 1-16.

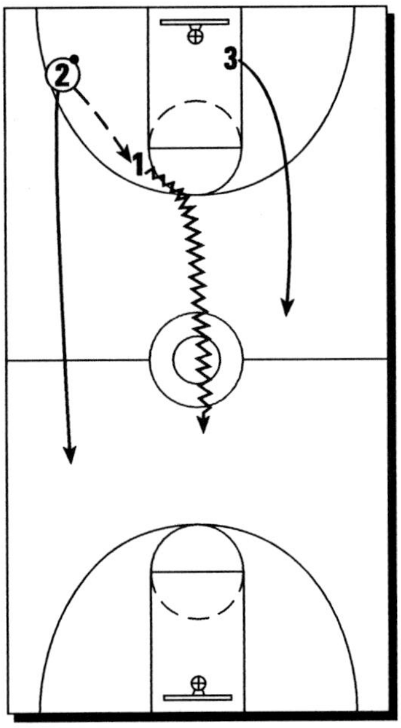

After four or five times, the offense can go long. You can also add a dummy defense and make it a little harder. A rule can also be established that if they don't get four out of five, they can't go long.

DIAGRAM 1-17. RECOGNITION DRILL

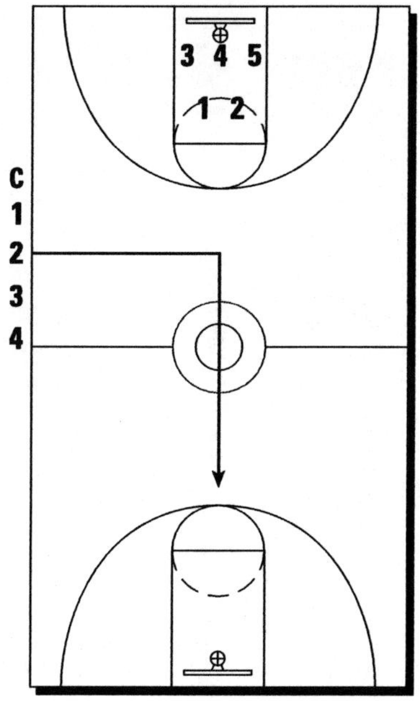

5/0. A coach calls a number and plays defense. The coach can call up to four numbers, but the offense always has an advantage.

DIAGRAM 1-18.

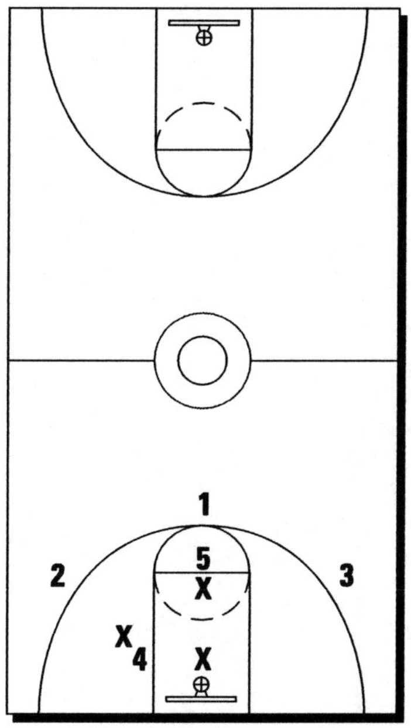

If you end up with 5/3, you want the reversal and the close-in shot. 5/1, you should score every time. 5/4 is a little harder, but you want them to recognize the numerical advantage, because someone is open. With us, if you have an uncontested 15-footer, we take it.

CHAPTER 2

TRANSITION BASKETBALL

JOAN BONVICINI

I'm here to talk about transition basketball and some things that I do to organize our program. One of the first things I do is to set up *goals* for the team. I have *10 offensive and 10 defensive* goals. You will have to adjust them to the level of your program.

OFFENSIVE TEAM GOALS PER GAME

- Shoot 51% as a team from the floor.
- Take a minimum of 70 shots.
- Shoot 70% from the free-throw line.
- Shoot 20 free throws.
- Get eight fast-break baskets.
- Get 12 offensive rebounds.
- Get 20 assists.
- Commit no more than 17 turnovers.
- Have no 30-second violations.
- Score at least 85 points.

DEFENSIVE TEAM GOALS PER GAME

- Hold opponents to 42% field-goal percentage.
- Allow a maximum of 60 shots.
- Allow a maximum of 15 free throws.
- Outrebound the opponent by five or more.
- Allow a maximum of 12 assists.
- Force a minimum of 20 turnovers.
- Force one 30-second violation.
- Take two charges.
- Get at least eight steals.
- Allow no more than 70 points.

I give these goals to each player, and they put them in their notebook.

Obviously, if we are going to play a tough opponent, I will adjust them before the game. We will put these on the board at halftime. Your *goals must be realistic* so you must adjust them to fit your level. On the other hand, as the season progresses, you can also raise them. It makes a big difference if you put them down as *team goals,* as opposed to individual goals.

Something else I did. Coach John Wooden had a Pyramid of Success. I made a little pyramid, too. At the bottom, I put all of our nonconference opponents, and I listed them. Then, at the next level, I listed all of our conference opponents. Above that, I put in the conference tournament and each level of the playoffs. The players really liked that. They would put up the pyramid in the locker room before a game, with the goals listed. This also went into the players' notebooks. Before the season starts, I make a chart of what I must cover for the season, and then break it down into week-by-week prior to the first game. Because of the shortening of our preseason, I tried to put in too much too soon. I learned a good lesson. We needed more fundamental teaching. So, I recommend that you keep it simple and then build on it as the season progresses.

Before the season starts, I put out a master plan and discuss it with the staff. This includes all the things I want to teach for that particular year. I list conditioning and fundamentals. Under fundamentals, I list *individual offense and individual defense*. Then, I list the team offenses and defenses, transition game, jump-ball offense, free-throw situations, out-of-bounds plays, and presses. Then, these must be put in week-by-week prior to the start of the season.

My main topic is *transition.* I always considered myself a fast-break coach; I was averaging about 80 points per game. When I put this in, we went to 90 points per game. What happened is that our pace is very difficult to defend. It's not like Westhead when he was at Loyola–Marymount. We worked at defense, too. Let's start at the beginning, the way I do it.

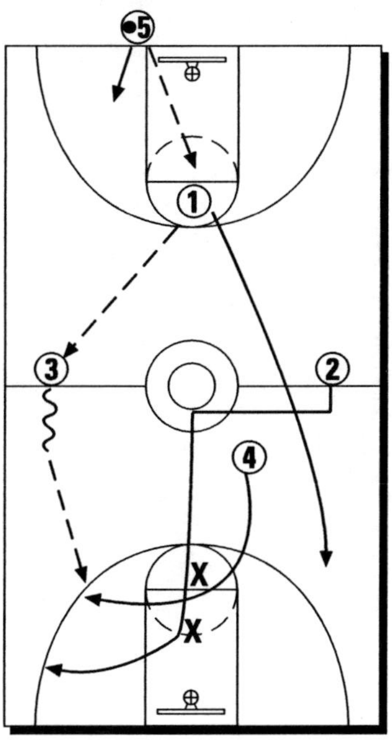

DIAGRAM 2-1.

5 takes the ball out-of-bounds. 5 must get the ball out of the net before it hits the floor; 5 then steps out- of-bounds and throws the baseball pass. 1, the point guard, starts about the free-throw line extended. The further you start the guard from the baseline, the faster she will get down the floor.

1 is in the middle of the court. 1 will make one or two dribbles and make a chest pass on the run to either 2 or 3. You don't necessarily use your best ball handler here because she is only going to make one or two dribbles. But, she must be able to make the chest pass on the run. 2 is on the left side of the court; 3 on

the right. No matter where they are when the ball is shot, *2 will always go on the left, 3 on the right.* They must be able to catch the ball on the run and should be good perimeter shooters. 4 is generally the big forward. As soon as the basket is made, 4 runs the middle of the floor and goes mid-post ballside. 4 will then reverse pivot.

DIAGRAM 2-2.

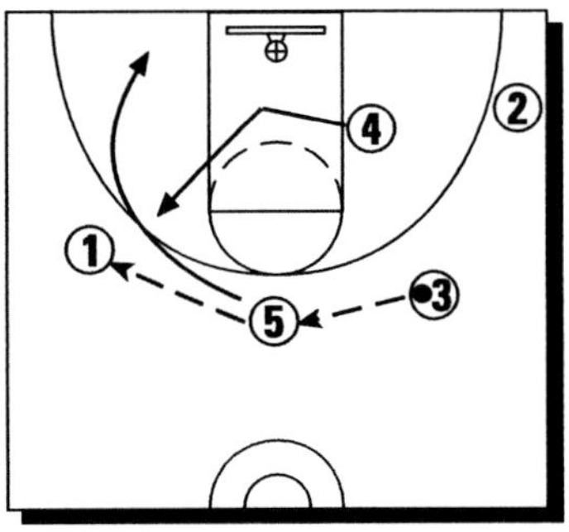

3 has the ball; 4 is on the block; 2 is in the corner; 1 went opposite and is spotting up on the weakside. 5 is the trailer. 3 can pass to 2 or 4, but in this case, reverses to 5 who passes to 1. 4 flashes toward 5 since 5 has the ball. 5 can shoot the three-pointer as an option. After 5 passes to 1, 5 cuts to the block. 4 fills the high post.

DIAGRAM 2-3.

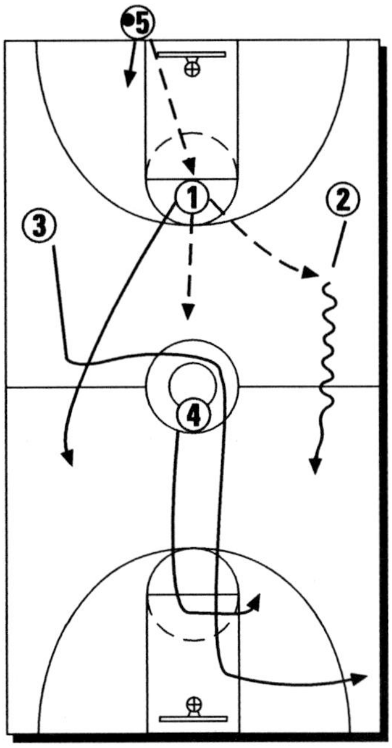

5 inbounds to 1, and 1 passes ahead to 2. 4 goes down the middle and posts up on the strongside block. 1 goes away. 3 cuts to the middle. 2 dribbles down the side. When 3 fills the middle, the cut to the ball must be a *direct cut.* The cut should not be on a *diagonal*, rather, an "*L*" cut should be made. 3 then goes to the corner. If 2 and 3 can't handle the ball, 1 should dribble down the middle until 2 and 3 spot up.

DIAGRAM 2-4.

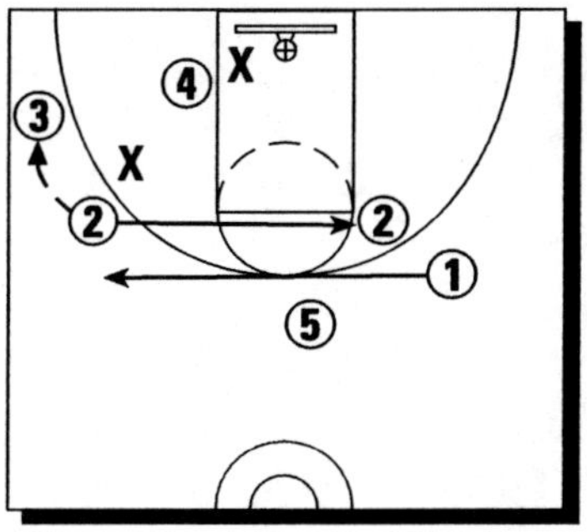

3 is in the corner, and you have a triangle with 2, 3, and 4. 2 passes to 3 in the corner. The defense must make a decision to guard either the corner or the post. 2 interchanges with 1. This keeps 2's defender from double-teaming in the corner.

DIAGRAM 2-5.

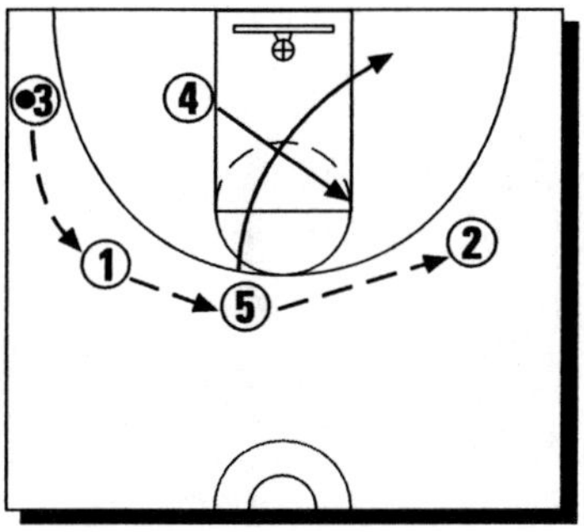

3 passes to 1, who passes to 5, who then passes to 2. 5 cuts to the low post; 4 comes high. *The person on the block is the number one option.* We want her to get the ball as often as possible. That's why we emphasize executing a strong reverse pivot. Some years I made 4 and 5 interchangeable.

DIAGRAM 2-6.

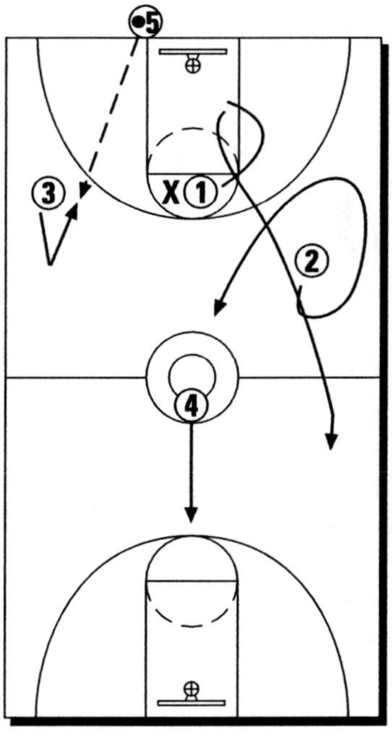

Let's say that 1 is guarded. 1 runs a *circle route* to try to get the ball. 3 and 2 have started to run, but it is important that they are not more than 15 feet from 1. When 2 and 3 see 1 being guarded, they come back. Suppose this time 5 passes to 3. 3 takes the ball on the dribble; 1 goes opposite; 2 goes middle. 4 posts up on the strongside block. If 5 has a strong arm, she can pass the ball to half-court to 2 or 3. When you run this system, your opponents will be so conscious of this: that instead of sending four players to the offensive boards, they will send three.

DIAGRAM 2-7. SKIP-PASSES

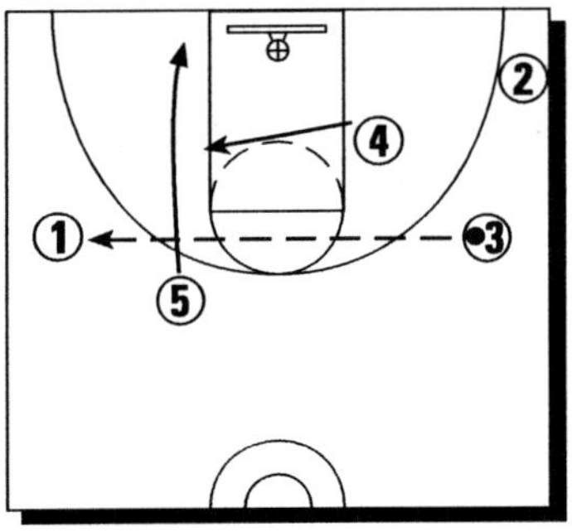

3 has the ball; 2 runs the turnout; 4 is on the block. Instead of passing to 5, 3 skip-passes to 1. If 1 has the three-point shot, she shoots it. 5 cuts to the block; 4 flashes high. 3 fills at the point. You must teach your team when this *transition ends* and when you start your *regular offense. It ends when you have a reversal and get nothing out of it.*

DIAGRAM 2-8.

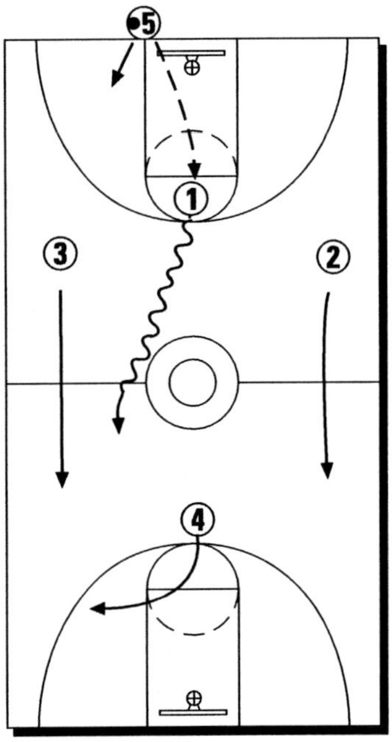

Assume that 2 and 3 are not open. 1 declares a side. 2 will remain opposite. 5 will come down and set a screen.

DIAGRAM 2-9.

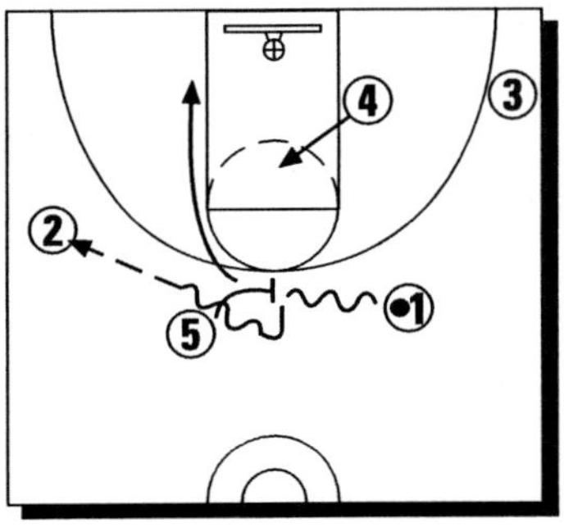

1 has kept the dribble. 5 sets a screen for 1 near the top of the circle and goes to the block. 1 could either have the jump shot, or can pass to 2 for the shot. 5 can also step back and get the pass back from 1. 4 then goes to the high post.

DIAGRAM 2-10.

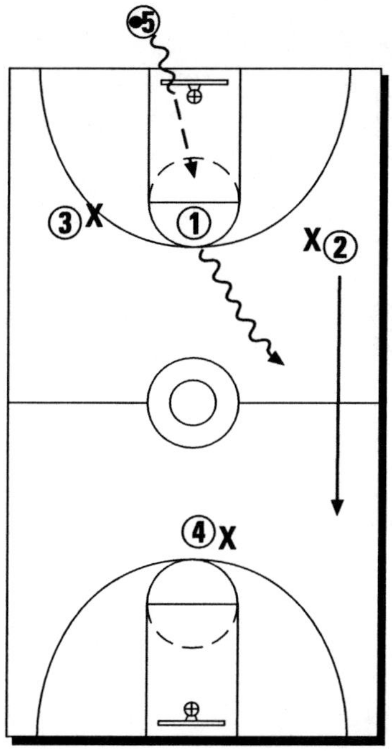

This diagram illustrates how opponents try to stop this situation. They allow the point guard to get the ball, and they defend 2, 3, and 4. It is very important that 1 declares a side and stays on that side. This makes the screen by 5 very important.

DIAGRAM 2-11.

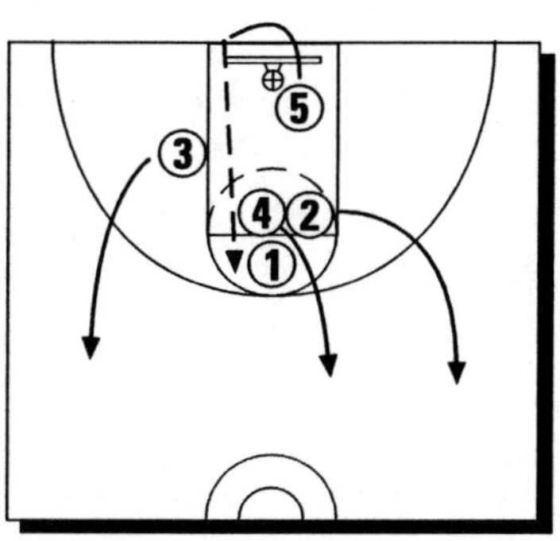

This is the way we practice the transition starting on the first day of practice. Prior to going out on the floor, I tell each person her position. Then, I diagram and go through the simple options in the beginning. Then, we will walk through it, stressing the importance of how 5 takes the ball out of the net. The point guard must start in the middle of the court. If 1 goes on the side, she takes away the option to the wing. I do 5-on-0 every single day. All five players are in the key. 5 puts the ball in the basket, and we break. I give them options and no defense, and require them to rebound all missed shots.

DIAGRAM 2-12.

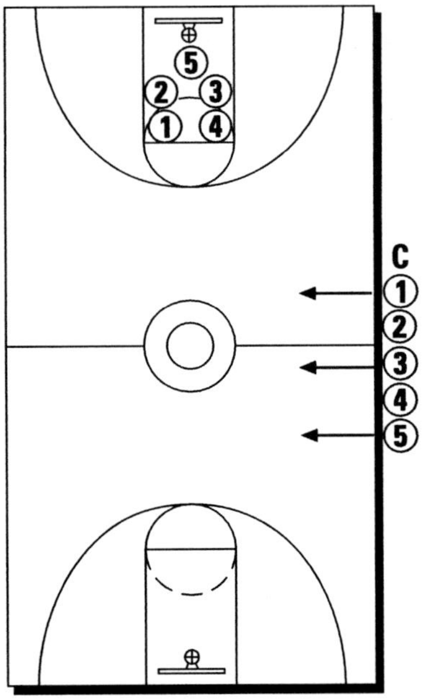

Then, we do 5-on-5. We have a coach near mid-court with five defensive players. She will send out three players, or four players or all five. They could be trapping, or could be challenging the point guard. We spend 10 to 15 minutes a day on this. *When don't we run transition?* On a dead ball, if it's a crucial part of the game, or at the end of a close game.

DIAGRAM 2-13.

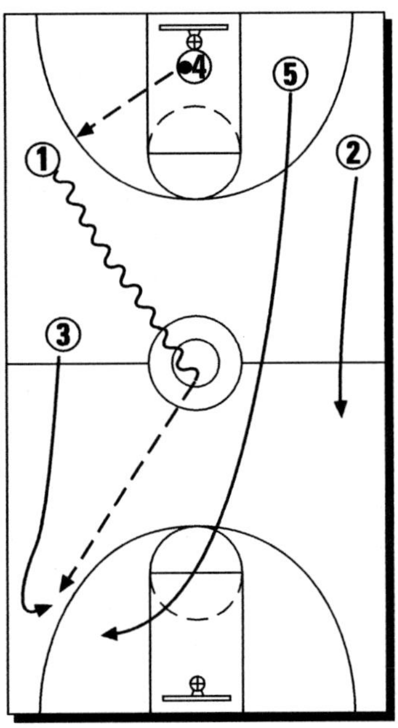

After a missed basket, we do the same thing. Suppose 4 rebounds and outlets to 1. 1 fills the middle, and 2 and 3 run wide. The player who didn't get the rebound, 5, goes to the block on the ballside. I like the fast break. It's fun to play and fun to watch. More kids are going to play, and they must be in shape.

DIAGRAM 2-14.

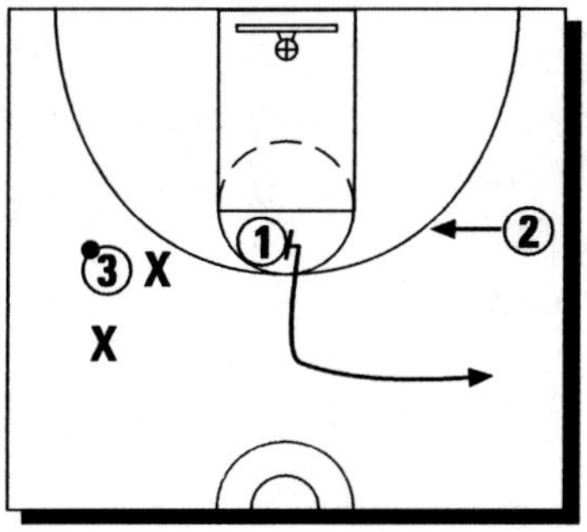

If you are being pressed and the ball is inbounded to 3, 1 goes away, and 2 replaces.

DIAGRAM 2-15.

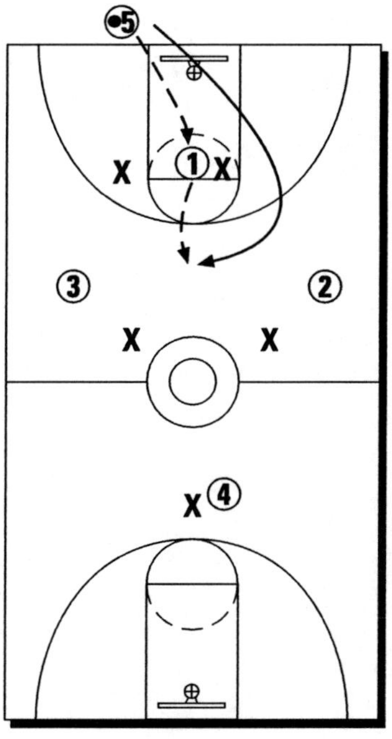

With this system, people are afraid to press you. But, let's say that they do press with a 2-2-1. 1 must come up to get the ball. 1 gets trapped. 5 does a semicircle, and I promise you, 5 will be open for the pass from 1. 2 and 3 are now open for the pass from 5. I don't let 5 dribble. 5 catches, jump stops, and passes to 2 or 3.

DIAGRAM 2-16.

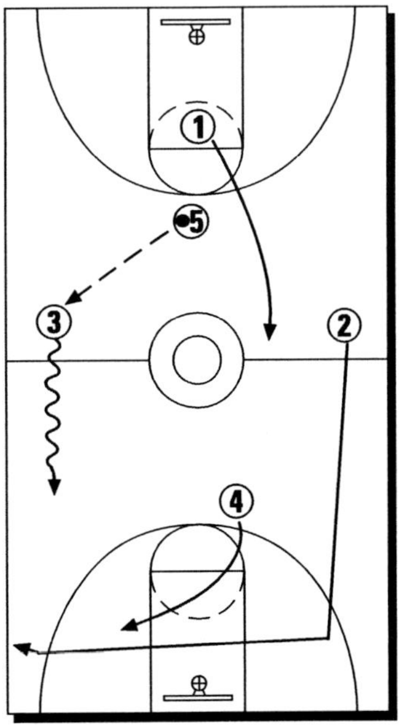

3 dribbles down; 2 does a *turnout;* 4 is on the block; and we are in the offense. I don't believe that you can run an offense like ours and then sit in a 2-3 zone on defense. I have always liked to *switch* defenses.

CHAPTER 3

DEVELOPING THE FAST BREAK

Jim Harrick

I think that we run as well as anybody, but I have never seen anyone teach the fast break part-to-whole. I've run John Wooden's fast break at all levels. I tell our players that the number one skill is listening. Number two, you better have good hands or I won't throw you the ball. When you get on the court, I want you to have five basic things. I call it the *"Big Five:"*

1. *Stance.* I want you in a stance at all times, feet as wide as the shoulders, chest out, back straight, head up, and bent at the knees — never at the waist. I don't think it makes a lot of difference how you hold your arms, but it does make a difference how you are in the rest of your stance.
2. *Concentration.* Concentrate on everything you do. When you get on the floor, give me everything you've got for a couple of hours.
3. *Quickness.* We work on quickness every day, both hands and feet. We want to be quick in everything we do. Be quick, but don't hurry. Have your players go as fast as they can under balance and under control.
4. *Balance* means that your head is at the mid-point between the two feet on everything that you do. If I am shooting, dribbling, rebounding, I want the head on the mid-point between the two feet. They say don't reach. What are they saying? Don't take the head out of the mid-point between the two feet. Balanced players play; unbalanced players sit. *Quickness and balance* are the two most important factors in basketball.
5. *Hard play.* I just came from an NBA tryout camp. We had one player who played so hard that it made everybody else look like they were standing still. He energized the others on our team.

THE SEVEN FUNDAMENTAL AREAS. We teach these aspects every day:

1. Acknowledge a good pass. When a player passes you the ball and you score, you thank him in some way.
2. The ball goes on the chest, under the chin, with the elbows out. While in the stance, I want the ball touching the chest. If you do that, no one will take it away from you.

3. The two-foot jump stop. When I stop while dribbling, I want a two-foot stop, balanced, under control, and the head at the mid-point ready to pass, or shoot. Make a two-handed pass. Then, fake a pass, make a pass.
4. V-cut and ask for the ball. Everything we do on offense starts with the V-cut. If the receiver doesn't ask for the ball, don't give it to him.
5. Step back and crossover on the dribble. This will eliminate the reverse pivot where someone can come from the weakside and steal the ball. Don't turn your back on the defense. Keep the ball no higher than the knee.
6. When the ball goes up, the hands go up. Make your players pinpoint the ball.
7. Follow the shot with your hands up.

Let's talk about building the fast break. In the NBA, the good teams all run, because you get easy baskets. Young players like to do it, and it teaches them to pass and dribble while on the move. It allows you to catch up when you are behind. Certainly you must control it, and you must be patient. You are going to have a few more turnovers. You must understand and teach good shot selection, and where the shots come from.

Why do we fast break? It teaches you to push the ball. It is the greatest conditioner of all time. If players cannot run the floor and change ends, then they are not able to go on to the next level. The most misused part of basketball is blocking out and transition defense. I want to score 1/3 of the time on my half-court set offense, 1/3 of the time from the fast break, and 1/3 of the time off of the defense. That makes you hard to beat. Before you can run, you have to rebound.

DIAGRAM 3-1. REBOUND, PASS OUT

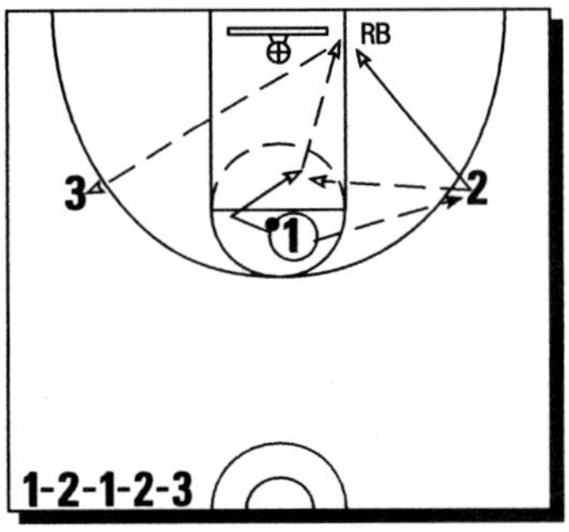

Each man must make a V-cut. 1 passes to 2. 1 fakes away and comes to the foul line and gets the return pass from 2. 1 then underhands the ball off the glass above the rectangle. 2 rebounds, and as he is coming down, he makes a half turn and makes the outlet pass to 3. We run this on both sides. The ball goes from 1-2-1-2-3.

DIAGRAM 3-2. TWO-LINE REBOUNDING

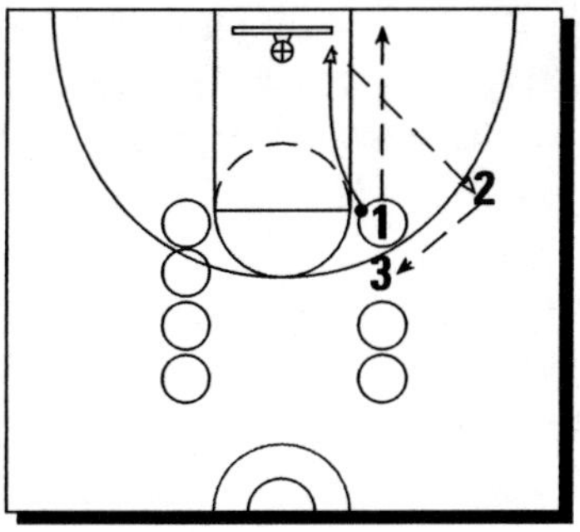

1 underhands the ball off of the board and gets his own rebound. He makes the outlet pass to 2, who passes to 3. The rebounder makes a half-turn while in the air. Run this on both sides at the same time. Change lines.

DIAGRAM 3-3. FLANKER

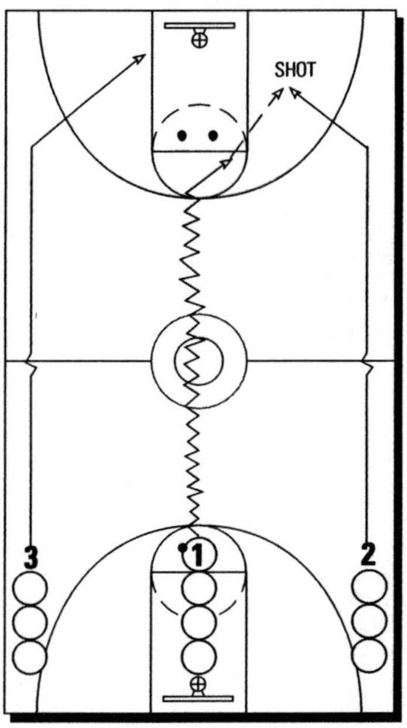

This is a technique fast-break drill. Go back to the seven fundamental areas. 2 and 3 go as fast as they can to half-court. There, they slow with balance and under control. Then, they go to the free-throw line extended, plant their outside foot, and go to the corners of the board in balance and under control. 1 takes three or four hard dribbles, and inside of the top of the key, he makes a two-foot jump stop. He can make the pass or shoot the jumper. After 1 makes the pass, he moves to the elbow on the side of the ball. He is ready to receive the return pass. The outside man usually shoots the bank jumpshot. The offside player goes to the block. He coils, hands up, ready to rebound.

DIAGRAM 3-4.

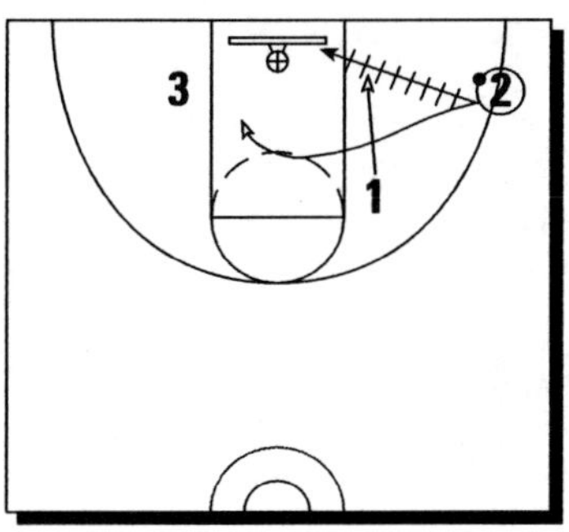

The shooter goes to the middle to rebound; 1 moves to the ballside block.

DIAGRAM 3-5. 4/0

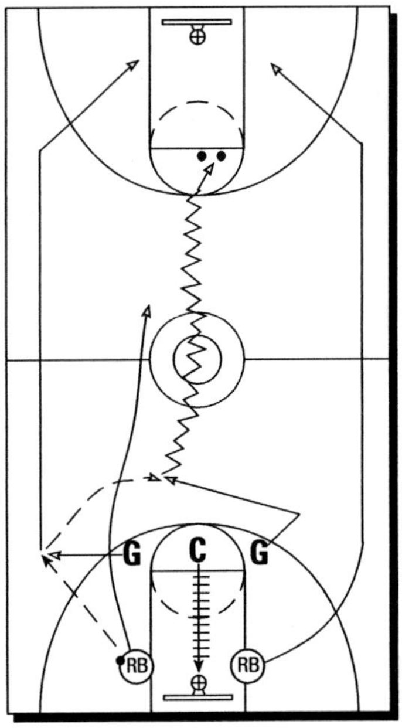

The coach shoots. Guards are responsible for the long rebound. The outlet pass is always made on the ballside. The rebounder is the trailer on the outlet side. The rebounder outlets to the ballside guard, and the pass is then made to the other guard breaking in the middle. The pass is made near the top of the key because there will always be a defender at half-court. The same principles apply at the other end.

DIAGRAM 3-6.

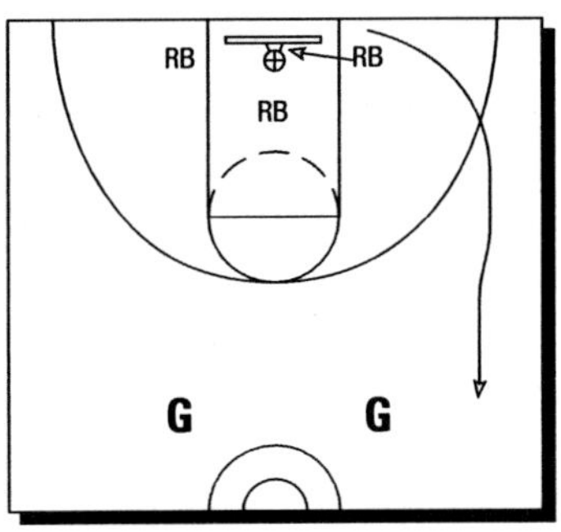

If you run it 5/0, the other big man will take the trail position on the ballside, and the rebounder will stop at half-court.

DIAGRAM 3-7. 3/2 CONDITIONER

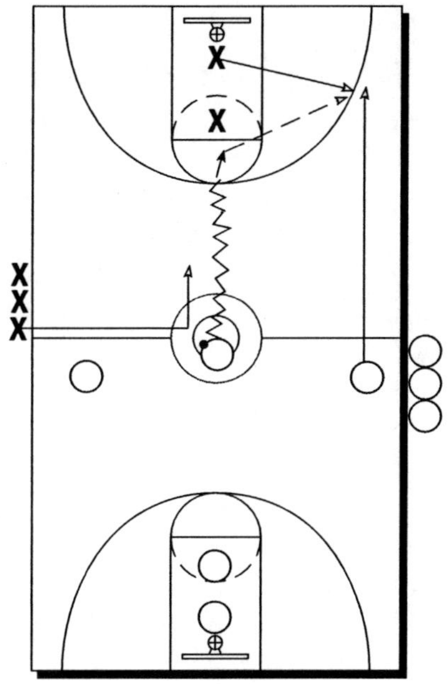

It is a 3/2 drill with a third defensive man coming in at mid-court, touching the floor, and then playing defense to make it 3/3. The back man takes the first pass; the front man takes the cross-court pass; and we hope our trailer picks up the reverse pass. That's how we defend the fast break. This is a continuous drill.

DIAGRAM 3-8.

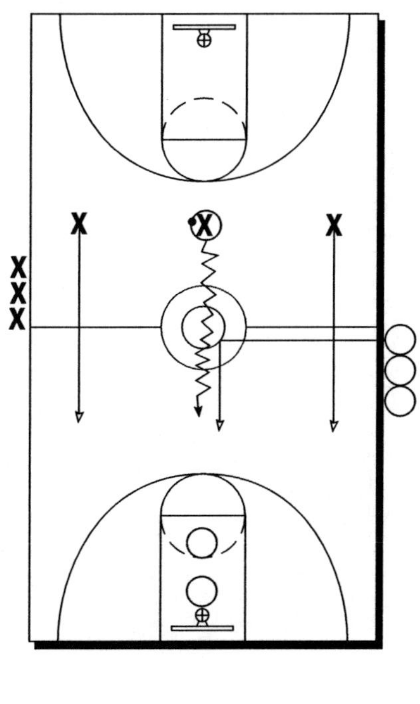

When the defense gets the ball either after a turnover or after a made basket, they become the offense and go to the other end where the same thing happens. The third man comes out to play defense as the offensive players cross mid-court.

DIAGRAM 3-9.

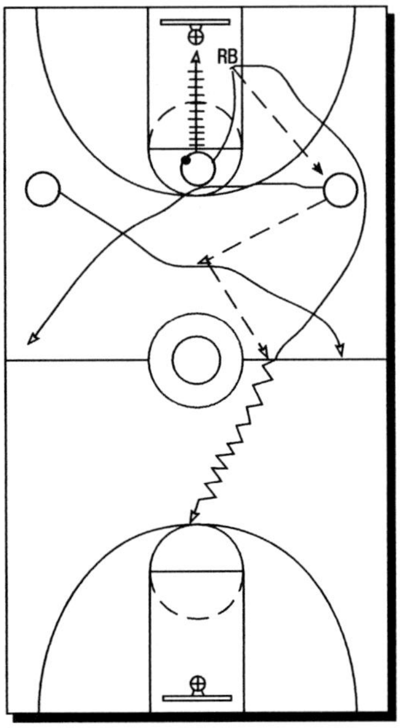

Three lanes; one weave. Rebound the ball off the glass and then make three bounce passes weaving to half-court. At half-court, the middle man makes one or two dribbles, and we are into the fast break. We do it so that each man has a chance to be in the middle. We do the same drill using a chest pass instead of a bounce pass. The third drill is a one-pass break. The ball is rebounded, and the outlet pass is made. Then, the ball is dribbled the length of the floor with the same fast break principles. The entire team goes one way; then, the entire team goes the other way. I don't like to have nine guys standing while three go down and back.

DIAGRAM 3-10. 2/1

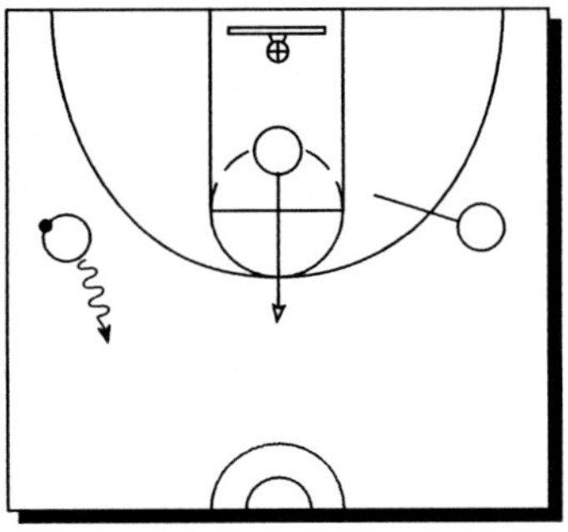

The middle man is the defense.

DIAGRAM 3-11.

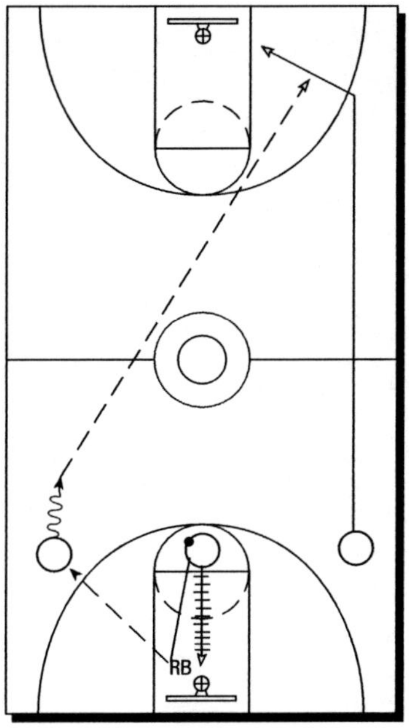

The ball is rebounded off the glass and outlet. The wing man makes a one-bounce dribble and makes a high lob cross-court pass to the other wing. This is not a baseball pass. It is a two-handed pass with a backspin that will go straight up when it bounces.

DIAGRAM 3-12. MIDDLE MAN BREAK

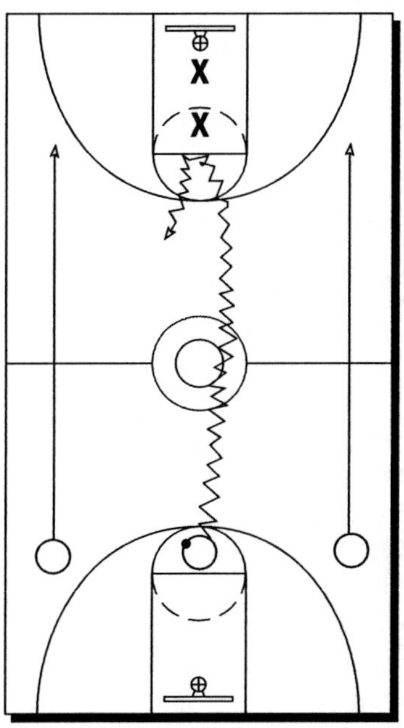

This is 3/2. When the defense gets the ball after a score or a turnover, the middle man remains in the middle and goes the other way on offense with the two other players. We run the middle man five or six times. He really pushes the ball up the floor.

DIAGRAM 3-13. COMBINATION, 5/5 BLOCK OFF, 5/3 BREAK

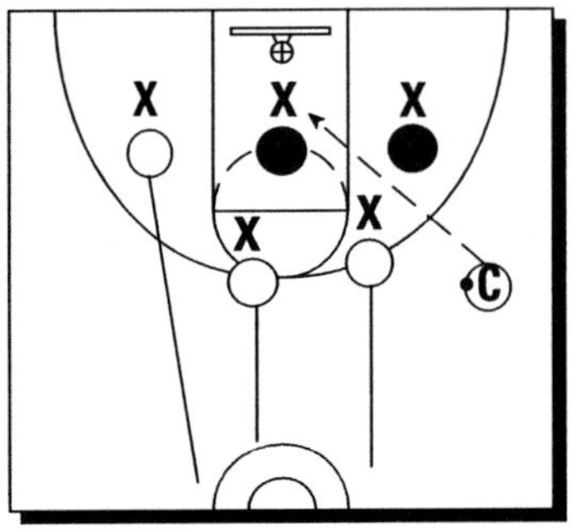

The coach says who does not play defense.

DIAGRAM 3-14. 4/2 CONTINUOUS

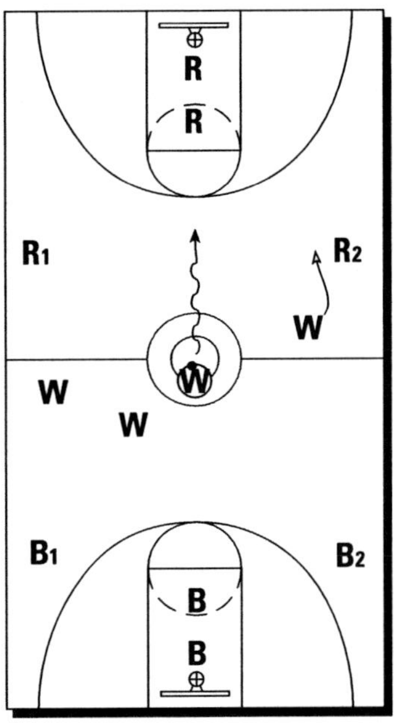

Three teams are involved — red, white, and blue. White starts with the ball at mid-court going 4/2. R1 and R2 are not in this. When you go 4-on-2, you should score. When red gets the ball after a make or a miss, then the red team goes 4-on-2 against the blue at the other end. B1 and B2 are not in this until the blue team gets the ball after a make or a miss. This is continuous action. The only bad thing about this is that it takes twelve players.

DIAGRAM 3-15. 5/5 CONTROL

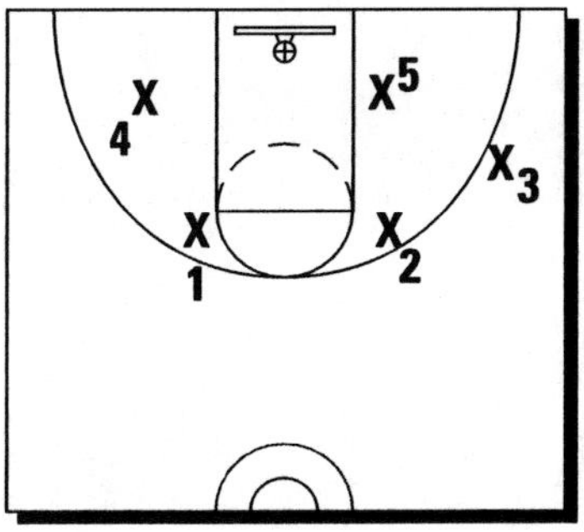

This is not a fast-break drill, but it is a fast-break drill. The numbers go man-to-man offense; the X's play man-to-man defense. If the numbers score, then they press. If the X's are scored on, they run the press offense. If the numbers don't score, then, they are in transition defense. If the X's stop the numbers, then they fast break. After we go down and back, we change. X's go on offense to start. Sometimes, we just let them go and scrimmage, but usually we control it this way. We also control the scrimmage with a time-and-score factor. We may start from a foul shot. You can do more teaching when you're in a 5/5 control situation. You are a teacher of basketball, and the court is an extension of the classroom. You have your methods, discipline, and know what you are doing. Teach what you know, and know what you teach. You win games by teaching from three to five in the afternoon. You don't teach during the games; you are coaching then. But, you are teaching 90% of the time. Don't get your priorities mixed up. Hopefully you will help your team win by covering all aspects of the game in practice.

CHAPTER 4

THE TRANSITION OFFENSE

JIM JABIR

We are going to talk about transition offense. The thing that you need to understand is that our transition offense is our offense. That's all we do. That's very important. We don't spend time running plays in a half-court offense. I got this from Paul Westhead when he was at Loyola Marymount. I want to start off of a *made* or a *missed shot.* This is a *numbered break* off of a made basket. The key is its *simplicity.* If your kids don't believe in this, it is not going to work. The whole premise is based on getting to a spot to shoot the ball faster than the defense can. You must be totally committed to running the floor as hard as you can every single time. When I started at Marquette, they hadn't won in about nine years, and we needed something different. Kids like to play this way, and I thought it would help our recruiting.

Secondly, we were playing teams who were better than us, and we needed a way to compensate for that lack of skill level. We want to make our opponents uncomfortable with our pace offensively, and we press for 40 minutes defensively. We want to take something away from you. We run the ball at you for 40 minutes every possession. A slow kid who is mentally trained to run hard, can run hard.

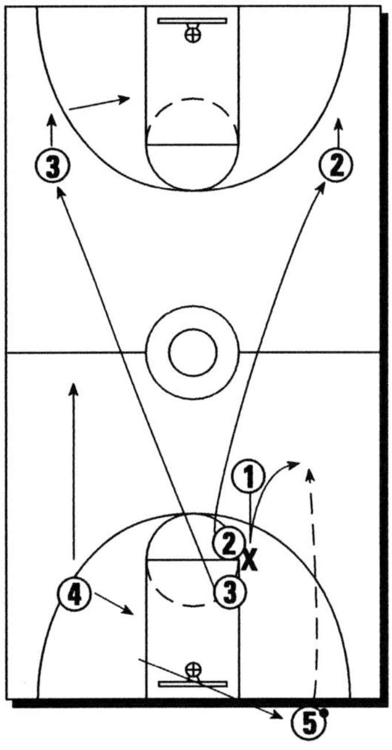

DIAGRAM 4-1.

Off of a made basket, 5 always takes the ball out of bounds. We teach a three-step out of bounds. We always go to the right side. We go left, right, and then left. You are turning and looking down the floor for the baseball pass. 1 is the only player who is allowed to bring the ball down the floor. 1 always goes to the same side of the floor. We teach either a *J-cut* or a jam cut. 3 is our best athlete. 3 goes to the basket well, and likes to drive and penetrate. As soon as we secure the rebound or the opponent has scored, she goes down the left sideline to the foul line extended and then she cuts hard to the basket. 2 is the glamour spot, the three-point shooter if you have one. She runs the right sideline and gets into a *ready-shot position.* 4 immediately goes opposite 1, outside the key where she is the safety. If 1 cannot get the ball, that's why 4 is there. We have an advantage when people press us. We got so good in breaking it that we had a numerical advantage at the other end. If 1 cannot get the ball, 4 comes back or else goes back for the ball. As soon as 4 receives the ball, 1 makes a cut into the middle for the pass from 4.

DIAGRAM 4-2. THE EARLY BREAK

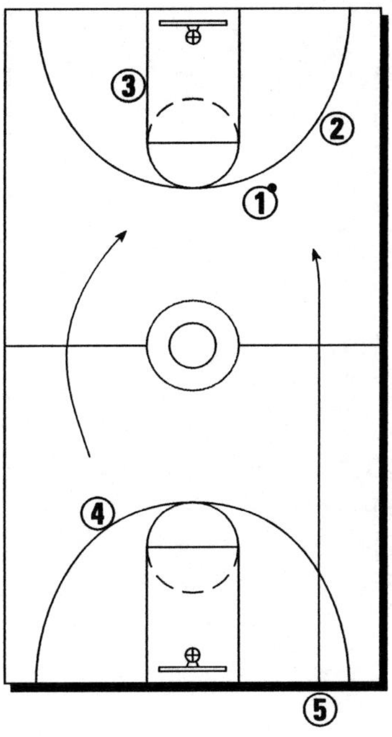

1, 2, or 3 is shooting the ball. It is either a layup for 3, or if she doesn't have a layup, she fans out. As soon as 1 catches the ball, she looks toward 3. We do not throw to 3. We throw to where 3 is going. 3 is running under the ball toward the basket. This spreads the defense. We talk a lot about dribbling north and south. We don't want to dribble from side to side. If 1 doesn't pass ahead to 2 or 3, she dribbles to the decision-making area, the right elbow. She only passes for a score. That's important. 1 has the advantage coming down the court because she is moving forward, and she should be able to go by you every time. If 1 can dribble in, she should do so. If not, she should pass to the open player. She should penetrate and pass out. She should force the defense to make a decision.

DIAGRAM 4-3. THE MIDDLE BREAK

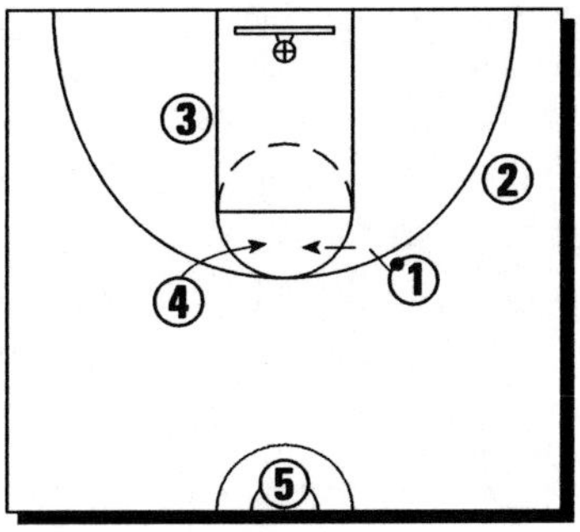

2 and 3 are not open. 1 has the ball at the elbow. 4 goes to the opposite elbow.

DIAGRAM 4-4.

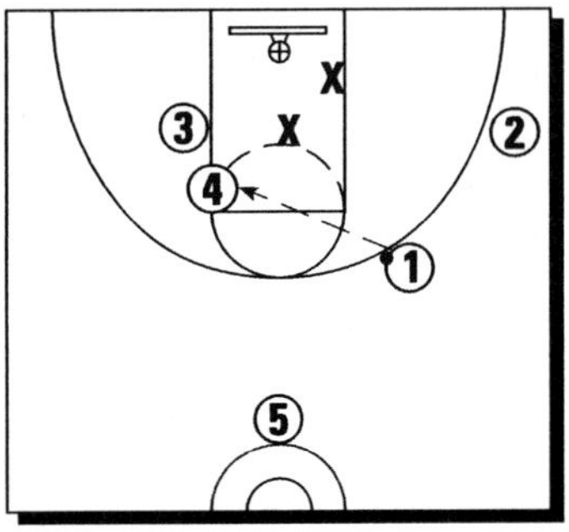

Usually a transition defense is trained to protect the basket. We call this the "key" pass, across the top of the key. 4 gets a lot of easy shots there.

DIAGRAM 4-5.

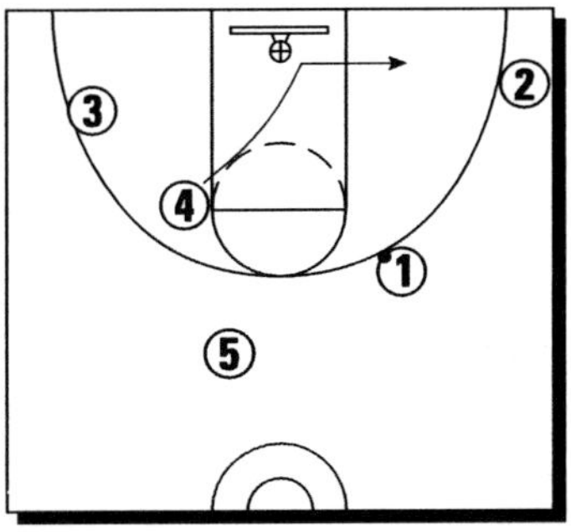

We have centers who can shoot the three-point shot. If 4 doesn't get the pass from 1, 4 drives to the block. The defense must respect that. 5 then fills behind 4, but stops at the top of the key at the three-point line. Most defensive centers aren't comfortable covering players on the perimeter, so we have an advantage.

DIAGRAM 4-6.

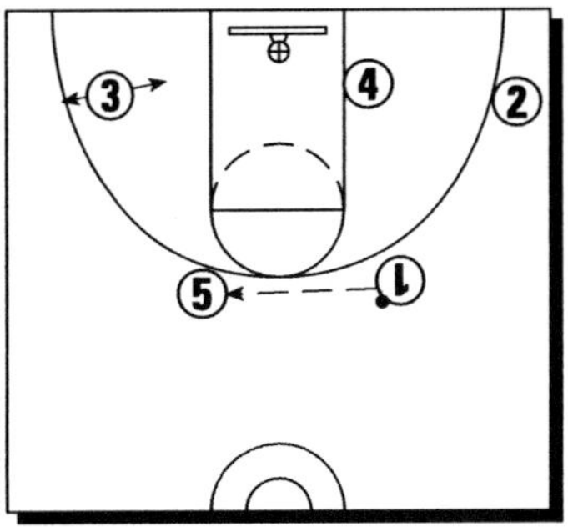

Now, we have the opportunity to go high/low with 5 and 4. We have an isolated 4 on the block. We spread the floor; 2 and 3 are three-point shooters, and 4 is isolated on the block. It is not important that you have three-point shooters. It is important that you make the defense spread the floor and make decisions.

DIAGRAM 4-7.

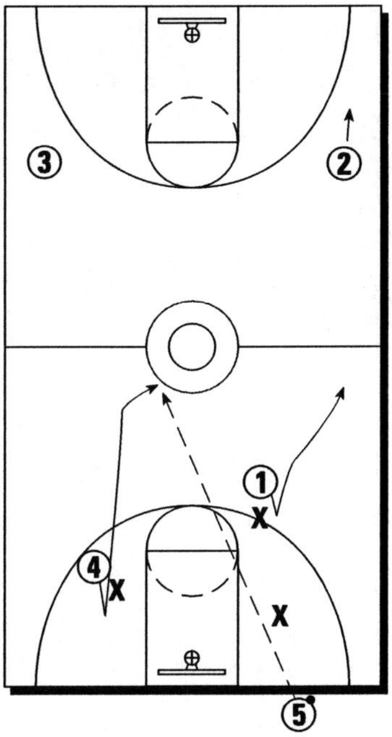

Let's be more specific on how we get open. On a made basket, 5 is out of bounds, 4 is opposite 1, and 1 is always on the right side of the floor. 2 and 3 are gone. 1 is face guarded, and 5's defensive player is off the ball. 4 takes one *jam step* toward the ball and goes long. We throw over the top to 4.

DIAGRAM 4-8.

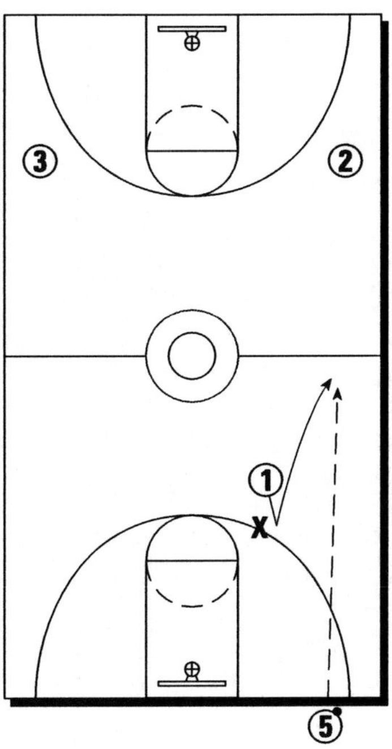

1 can use the jam step if she is face guarded. 1 takes one step into the defender and breaks long for the lob pass over the top.

DIAGRAM 4-9.

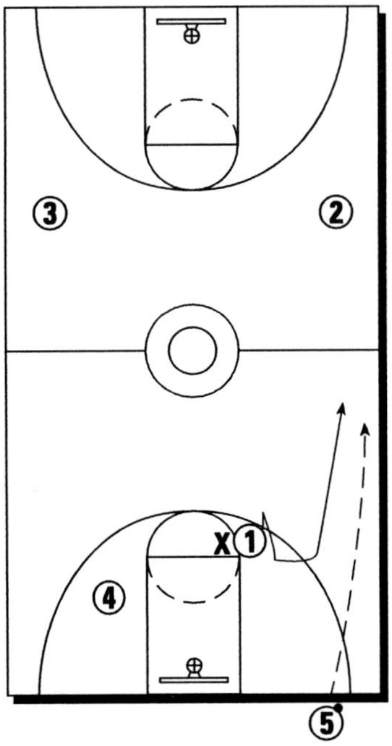

If 1's defender is on the side, we use the *J-cut.* 1 breaks toward the sideline and then goes long. We throw over the top to 1. The second time we play someone, teams stop pressing us. Do we have turnovers? Yes. We probably turn it over more than most of you are comfortable with. That's part of this system.

Here are some of our breakdown drills.

DIAGRAM 4-10. THE C-1-3 DRILL

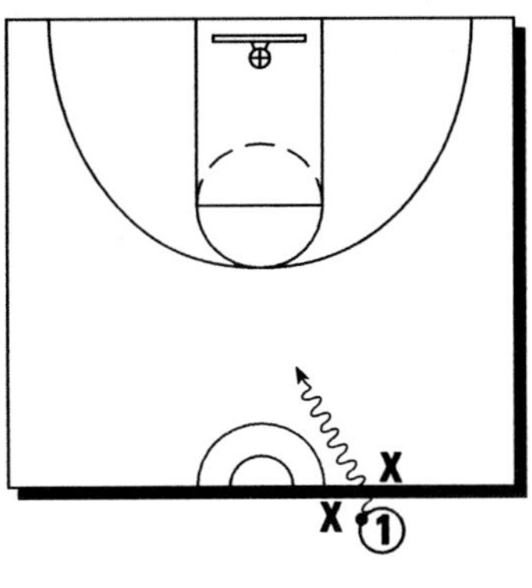

Our three players will simulate the top trap of a press. The coach takes it out of bounds and passes in to 1. 1 works on splitting the trap. Remember, in our system, 1 is our *press breaker.* We want 1 to catch the ball, turn, and look downcourt. At that point, we want her to *freeze* her inside defender. We don't want her on the sideline because the sideline acts as a defender. We want 1 to dribble right at the inside defender as hard as she can. 1 will go through the legs, behind the back, etc., and go by the inside trapper. She should not go sideways very long; she should go up the court.

DIAGRAM 4-11.

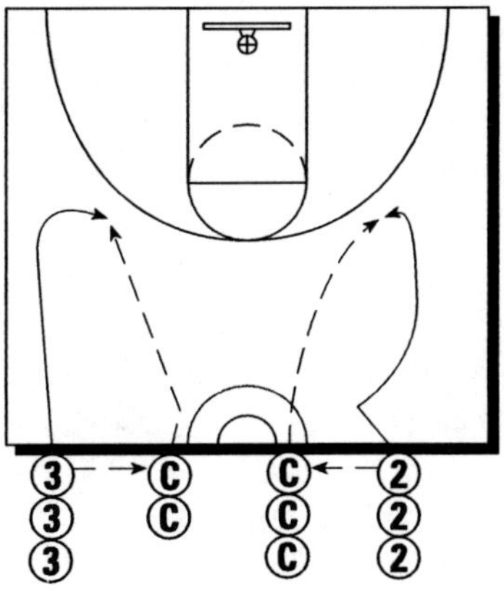

2's line up at half-court, pass to the coach, and run at top speed to a spot and get into a *ready-shoot* position. What I mean by a ready-shoot position is that my outside foot, furthest from the ball is pointed to the basket. This player then opens up to the point guard with hands ready to receive the ball. 2 will indicate she wants the ball by showing the *target hand.* 2 will catch the ball and turn the entire upper body toward the basket. The reason we shoot this way is simple. We want a *consistent shot.* The shooting arm hasn't moved, but the entire body is moving toward the basket. 3's will be on the other side running the lane, passing to the coach. The coach leads 3 to the basket. 3 works on her moves — a reverse, a pull-up bank shot, a *slide-by* shot, a 1-on-1 move to the basket. Sometimes, we have 3 rebound 2's miss. Most of 2's rebounds will go *weakside.*

DIAGRAM 4-12. THE C-2-4 DRILL

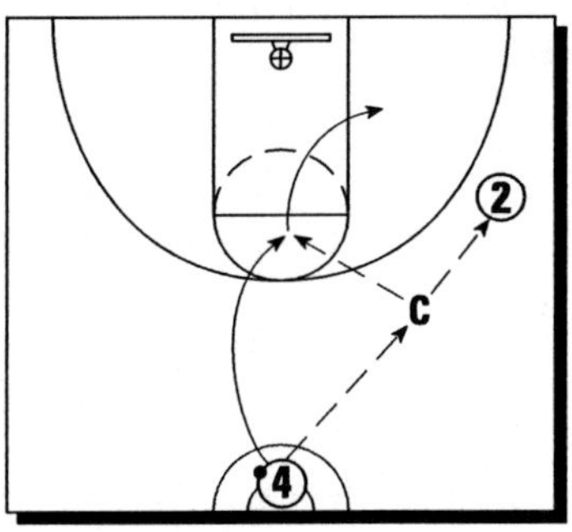

4 passes to the coach and fills into her area. Coach either returns pass to either 4 or 2. 2 can also pass to 4 and then move to an open spot so the ball can be kicked back out.

DIAGRAM 4-13.

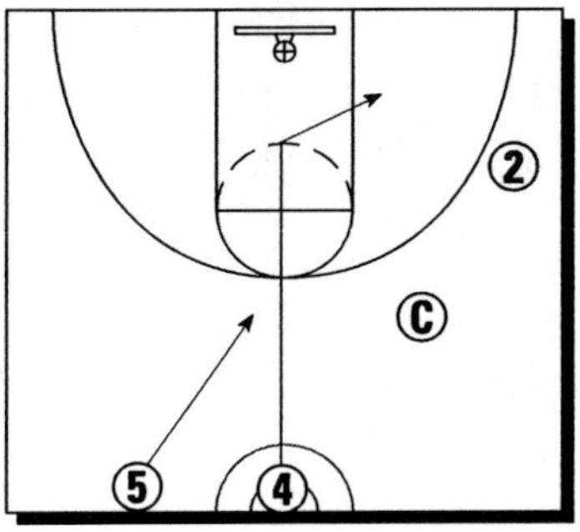

Later, we include 5 following 4, and we work on the high/low. We are taking our offense and breaking it down to its most basic parts.

DIAGRAM 4-14. THE TRANSITION DRILL

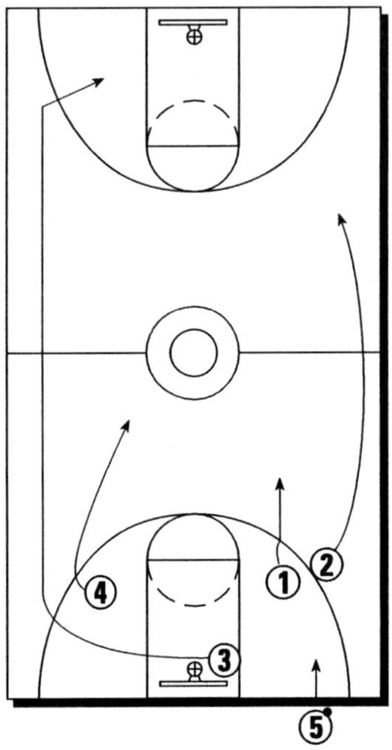

This is a great conditioning drill. We call this *"2-1/2 by 12."* One time down the floor is a half-cycle. So five times down the floor is 2-1/2 cycles. Everyone gets a shot. We time this and keep score. If we go 2-1/2 twelve times, that's 60 possessions, 60 shots. If you average one point per possession, you are doing well. Last year we averaged 80 possessions/game. 3 puts the ball in the basket and runs her lane. 2 runs her lane. 5 takes the ball out of bounds; 4 is the safety; and 1 goes. The first thing we look for is the *quickest shot*; that's the 5-1-3 pass for the layup. 5 must get the ball out of the basket and take the ball out of bounds at the other end. Now, we go the other way, and it is 5-1-2. If 2 misses, the ball is rebounded and passed to 1 to go back the other way. Everybody rebounds except 2, who is back on defense. If 2 hits, 5 takes it out. We do this five times. Then, another team takes over.

We have 15 kids on our team, three groups. We change people around to see what combination is the quickest. This system lends itself to offensive rebounding. When your 3, 4, and 5 run hard, the defense hasn't established itself yet. They have a much easier way to the basket because the defense isn't set. This system will not work if you don't rebound offensively. You can't take a shot and have three people watching at half-court. Also, in this drill, you are catching the ball in a game-speed situation. We are sprinting up and down the floor, so it is important that you have a conditioning program that will support this type of game. If you do this, your feet are going to hurt, your legs are going to ache. But when you see what it does to your opponents, it will be worth it.

This is something called *meltdown.* This is a phrase coined by Coach Westhead. When you are playing a team that is not accustomed to playing this way, there comes a time when they hit a wall and it is obvious. Halftime is not enough time to recover. When we play teams, we see their entire bench. This is one of the strengths in what we do. Now, you are playing against people who usually don't play because you are pushing the regulars to the point where they don't feel comfortable and can't run as well as they want to. Their reaction time increases. If you can get it in your kids' minds that this is all we are going to do, but we are going to do it hard, work on it, and execute it perfectly, you will score a lot of points off of it.

Is there a downside to this? Coach Westhead presses to create tempo. You are giving the other team more possessions too so you must score on your possessions.

DIAGRAM 4-15.

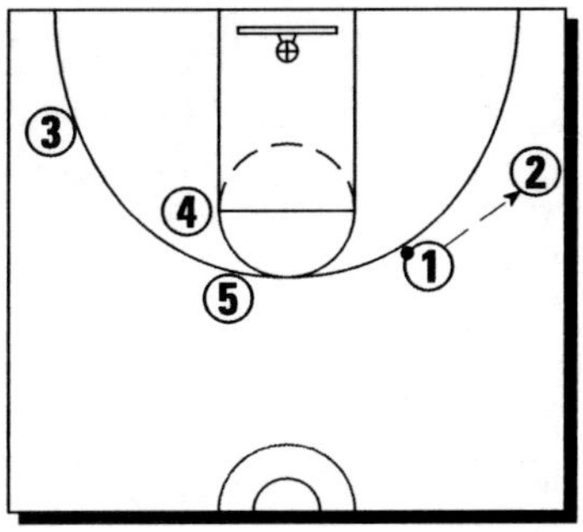

If 2 can run down, catch, get set, and shoot the same three-pointer, she would out of a half-court offense after 10 passes. Then, that's a good shot. I must convince my 3, 4, and 5 to rebound the misses at this pace; we have an advantage. One of the things about this system is because of the large number of shots, your opponent's lead isn't safe and neither is yours. I've gotten a little smarter where I will pull the ball out a little. Coach Westhead would tell you that you don't want to do that because you are sending a mixed message to your team. Westhead is so into the *mental aspect* of this that he says you can't go back and pull it out. But, if I have a 20-point lead with six minutes left, I'm not going to keep shoving it down their throat. I don't think you can even call this a fast break. It's beyond that. We run a lot of traps and presses to get the tempo of the game where we want it.

DIAGRAM 4-16.

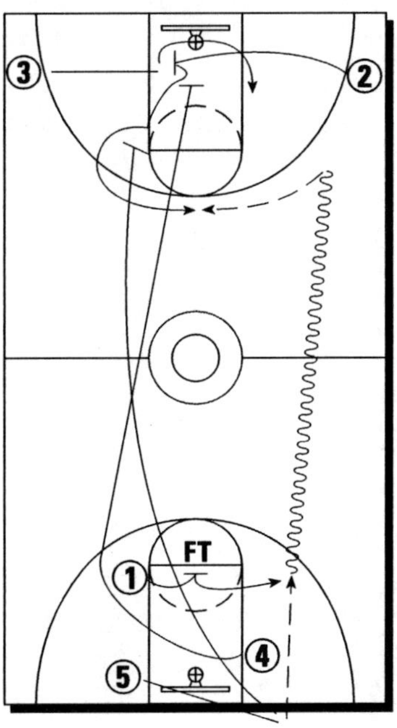

When our opponent is shooting a foul shot, we keep 2 and 3 at the other end of the floor. 1 takes the shooter. 5 takes the ball out of bounds, and inbounds to 1. At that point, we are in our *basic set* except that 2 and 3 are already down the floor. 2 screens for 3 who posts. 4 and 5 set *staggered screens* for 2. 1 passes to 2 for the three-point shot. We call this *"Two Double."*

DIAGRAM 4-17. LAST LEG

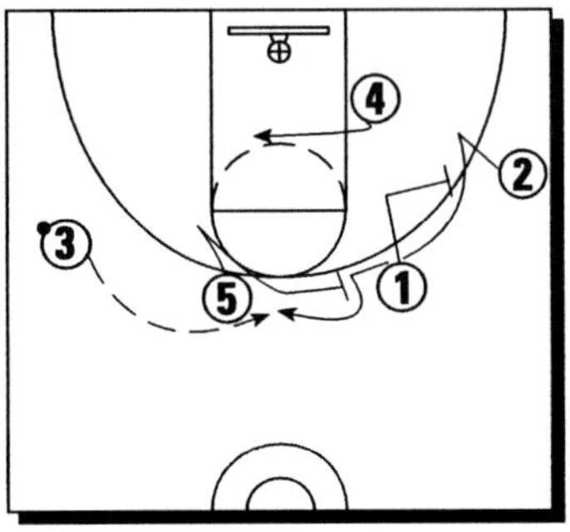

Every time the ball goes to 3, we automatically run this play. 1 passes to 5 and sets a screen for 2. 5 passes to 3 and sets a *staggered screen* for 2. 4 rolls inside. 2 comes off of the screens for the pass from 3. You have an inside game with 4 isolated low, and the best shooter coming off of a doublescreen.

Question: Does this work as well against a zone?

Answer: If we are running as hard as we can, we shouldn't be able to tell what defense they are playing. We do have a zone offense that we will use at times. But we try to run this first. Again, this is right out of our late break. If we were playing against a 2-3 zone, we would shade our players to screen the top two players of the zone. Everyone rebounds but 2.

DIAGRAM 4-18.

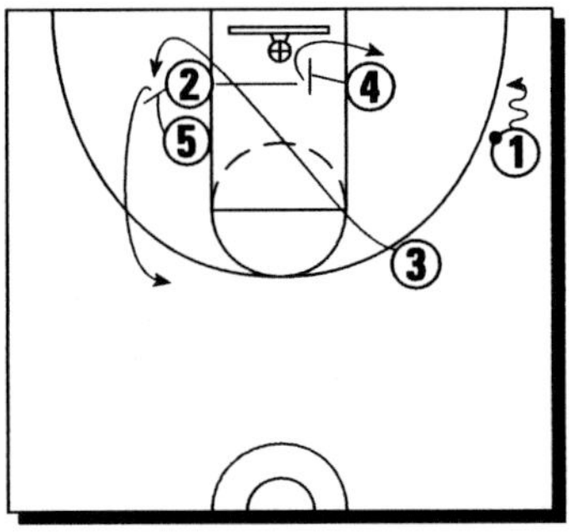

This is more of a setup. *2 goes through.* 1 dribbles at 2. 2 goes at 4. If her defensive person is on her side, she goes through. If the defense is behind, she curls. Let's say that she goes through. 4 screens. 5 screens down for 3; 3 goes high. All we have done is establish a triangle. We have set up the framework where our kids can go 1/1 or get a quick jump shot.

DIAGRAM 4-19.

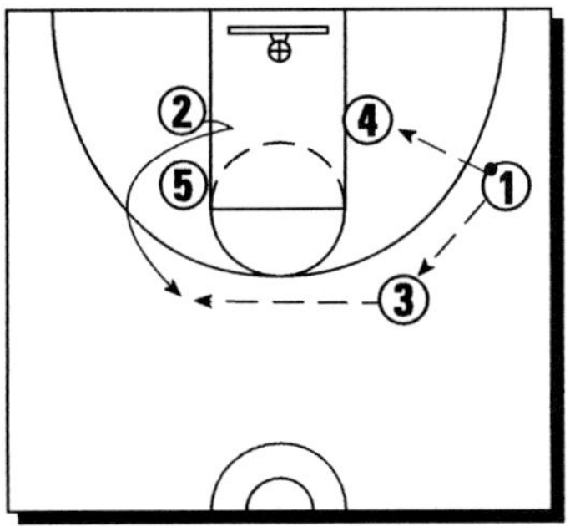

It looks like this. 1 has the ball. 4 is posting. 3 is at the top of the key and should be open because she came off the screen. 2 comes off the screen for the possible jump shot. The ball goes from 1-3, 1-4, or 1-3-2.

DIAGRAM 4-20.

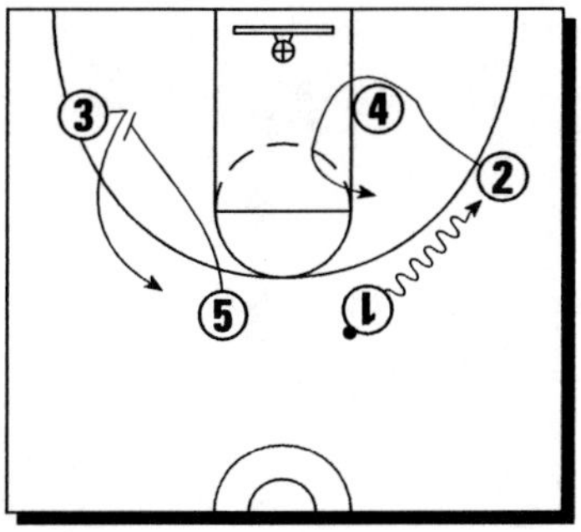

If 2 curls, 2, 4 and 1 would be in the triangle. 5 screens down for 3. We will call one of these plays in a time-out.

DIAGRAM 4-21.

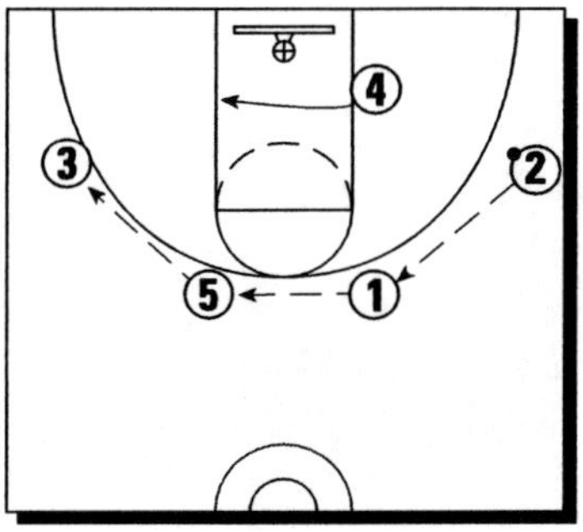

We usually end up with four out and one in. This is *Four Roll.* 4 shadows the ball.

DIAGRAM 4-22. REBOUND DRILL

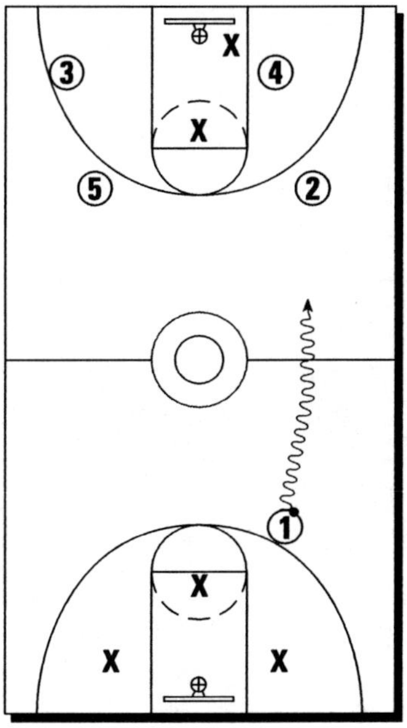

We have two defenders on one end, three on the other. We run two and 1/2 cycles against defenders. This is really a rebounding drill. We should get a good shot in this situation, but everyone goes to the board. If we miss, we don't shoot. We outlet it to 1 and go the other way for a quick shot and an offensive rebound if necessary.

CHAPTER 5

THE FAST BREAK SYSTEM

Muffet McGraw

I'd like to talk about just running; reasons to run and why people like to run. When I was a player I thought it was a lot of fun. The fans like to watch it, and the kids like to play it. So, the running game is the way to go in basketball. That's the future of basketball. I think it makes people work harder on defense if they know when they get the ball, they can just go. Kids are impatient when it comes to offense.

What kind of team do you need to run? If you're fast, it helps. But, I don't think you need to be quick; it's a mental kind of transition game. Some people think that there are two parts, offense and defense, and transition is getting down the floor between the two. You must make them get a mental attitude about running. They don't have to be that fast, but it's the first few steps that count. It's how quickly do they fill the lanes, not how fast they run. If you are going to run, you must be able to rebound because that is the key to running the break. If you can't rebound, then you must run on made shots.

Do you want to run a patterned break or just fill lanes? There are advantages to running the *patterned break.* For one thing, it helps everyone else on the team. It's good for you to know what spot you are in, but it is even better when all five know what you are going to do. You can place your players to take advantages of their individual talents; for example, you may want to put your left hander on the left side of the floor. The problem is when you play man-to-man you can't dictate where you are going to end up, so you need communication between players. It's easier for the rebounders and the point guard when you run a patterned break. It's more organized, and it helps with shot selection also.

One of the biggest things is just an expression, but it says exactly what you want your kids to do when they get the ball. *"Clear the ball."* All that means is all the things we used to say: get your elbows out, pivot, protect the ball, etc.

We don't want to be overly aggressive with the elbows, but we say *"point your elbow to the nose."* We bring the rebound to a point where the arms are horizontal, shoulder high with the elbows out. This eliminates a lot of jump balls and traveling. Same thing when you get the ball on the block. If you are good, you are going to get double-teamed. If you put the ball on the floor, the ball will be gone. Make a quick move, *"clear the ball."*

The *box-out.* We don't rebound as well from the zone as from a man. The thing I like about man is that when someone gets a rebound, you know whose man that is.

But, I realized that we didn't work in practice on blocking out from a zone. The biggest problem we had was that the wings always had two people, usually because the guards never blocked out. We work on the guard blocking out, but when they get beat, the forwards have two people, and you must work on that too.

DIAGRAM 5-1.

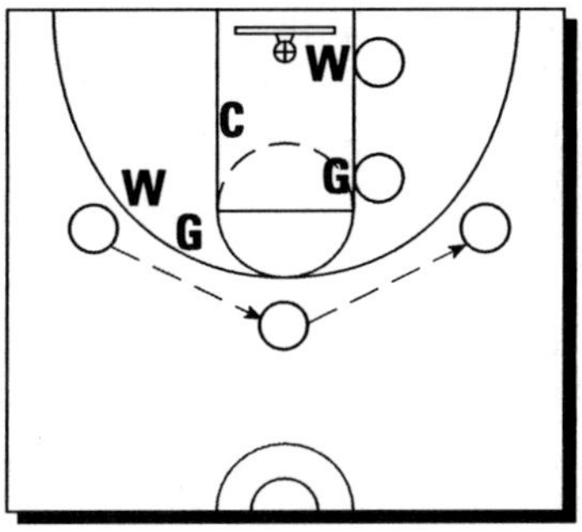

There are times in a zone when the ball is reversed when the guard can't get there.

DIAGRAM 5-2.

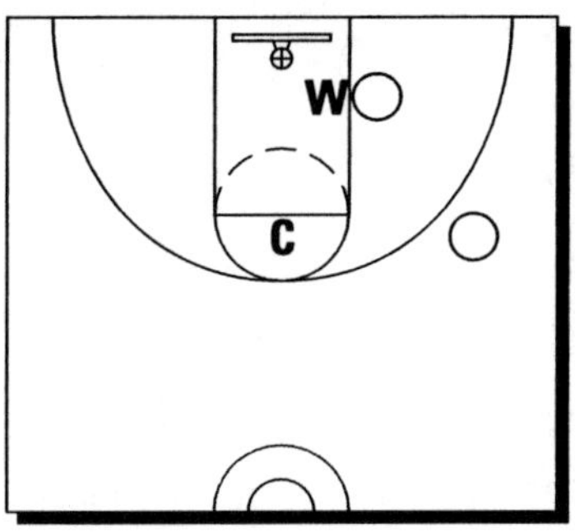

We got beat on the wing. We had a player on the wing and another on the block. The coach shoots the ball, and the wing first blocks out the person on the block and then should be aware of this other person coming from the wing. You must go get the ball; you can't wait for it.

DIAGRAM 5-3.

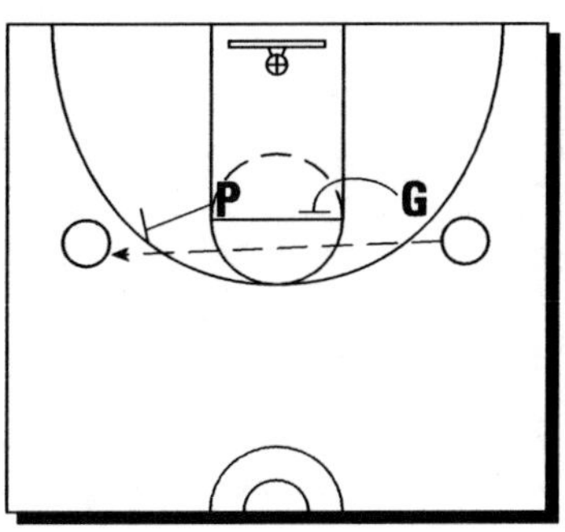

We do the same things with the guards. We try to emulate game conditions, for example, the *skip pass.* The shooter must shoot, and the guards must get there to block out.

DIAGRAM 5-4.

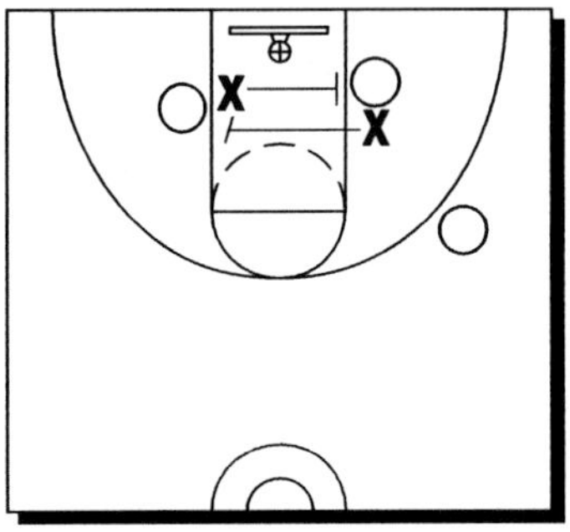

If you are fronting the post, you can't block out the post. So, we switch on the rebound by rolling to the opposite block. The help person blocks out the post.

DIAGRAM 5-5.

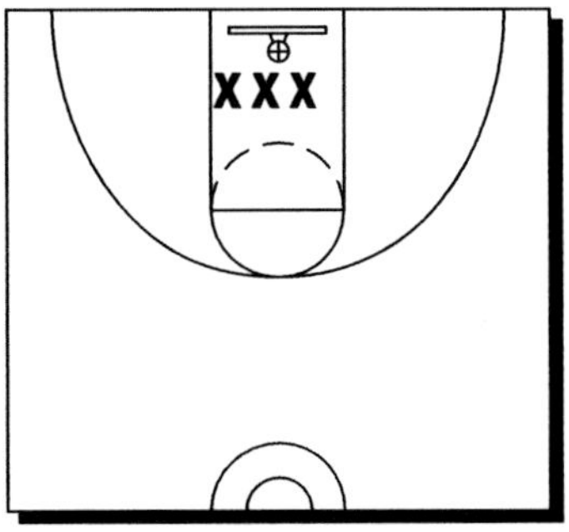

Put three people in the middle; three rebounds and out. We use the *"bubble."*

DIAGRAM 5-6.

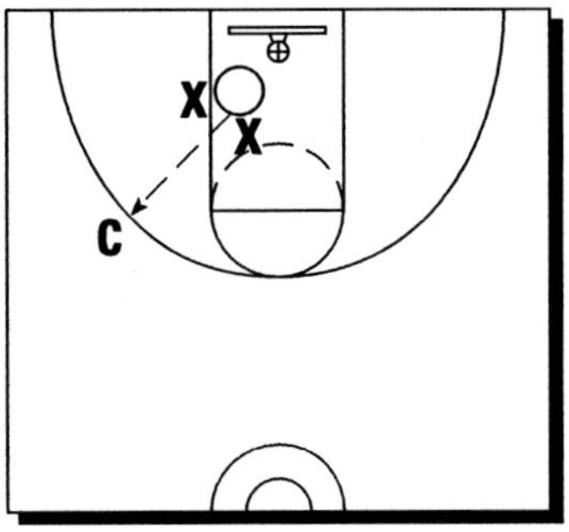

Getting more into the break, the thing we did to rebound was to put two people on the rebounder. The rebounder would outlet to the coach. We don't want them to dribble.

DIAGRAM 5-7.

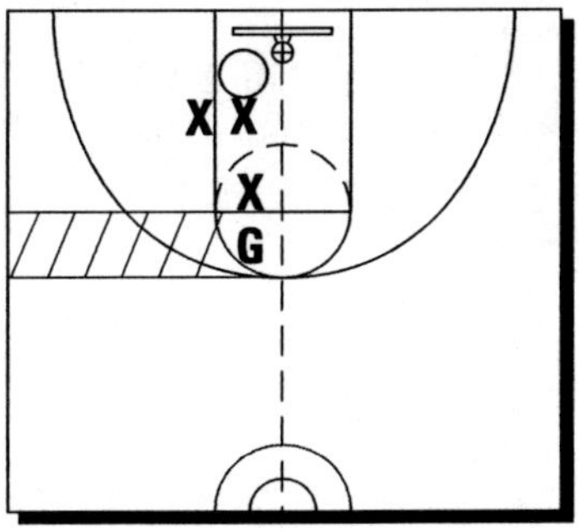

We then add the point guard with a defender on the point guard. She can only use half the floor, and we want her to get the pass in the area from the foul line to the top of the circle. We only outlet to the point guard. If possible, she should have her back to the sideline. In this position, she can see the entire floor. We never let them go long. They never catch the ball over their shoulder running down the floor. Run from side to side. If you happen to get the ball in the middle of the floor, look to the outside immediately.

DIAGRAM 5-8.

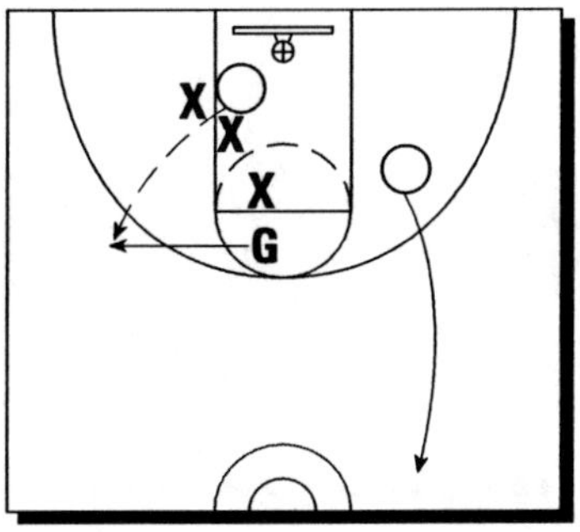

We then add another player to run the lane.

DIAGRAM 5-9.

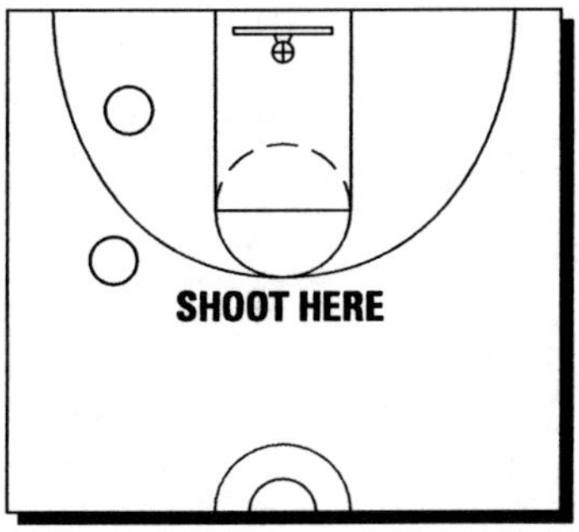

Shoot it from here or here. If you can't use the backboard, don't shoot it.

DIAGRAM 5-10.

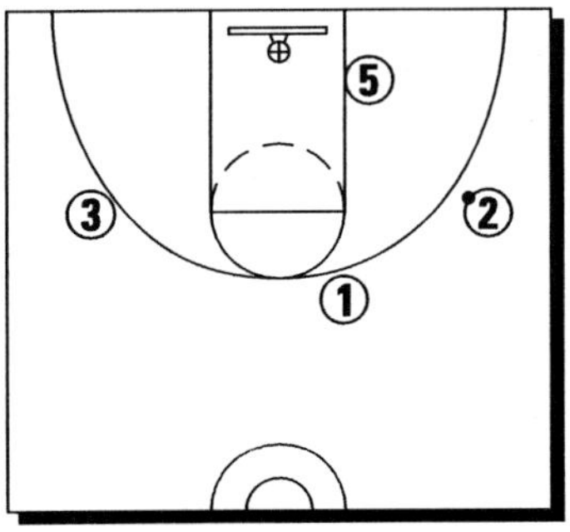

So, we finish the break like this. If the guard must be smart, the big people must be strong — big people who look for the defender.

DIAGRAM 5-11.

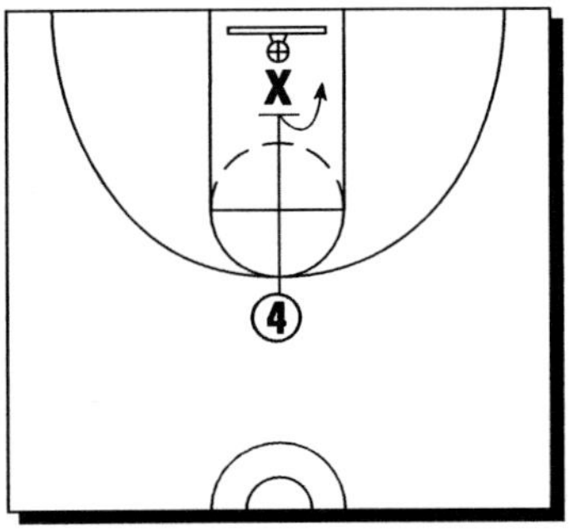

If it is a guard, run right into her face.

DIAGRAM 5-12.

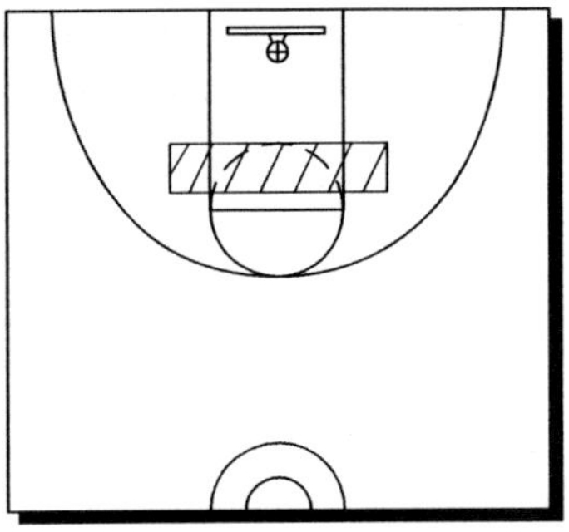

We tell the second trailer to run to the open spot. This area is open for the second trailer many times. We get a lot of jump shots in this area.

DIAGRAM 5-13.

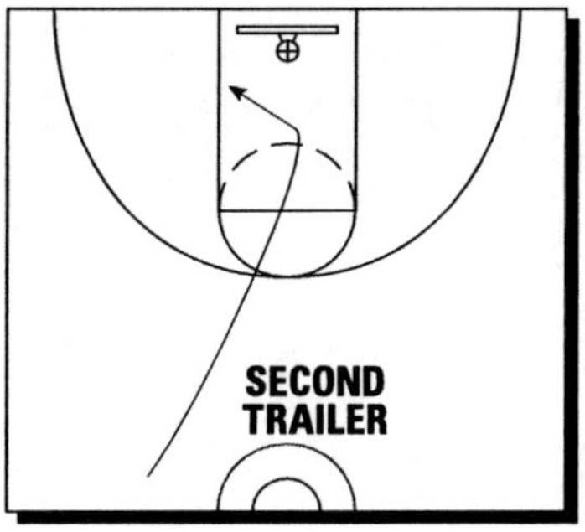

Don't have them run straight down. If they don't get the ball, veer to the block. They can't run like robots. I think it's an issue for women because they don't play on the playgrounds much. They are always in a structured situation when they play. They don't just play. They want to know where they are supposed to go.

TEACHING POINTS:

DIAGRAM 5-14.

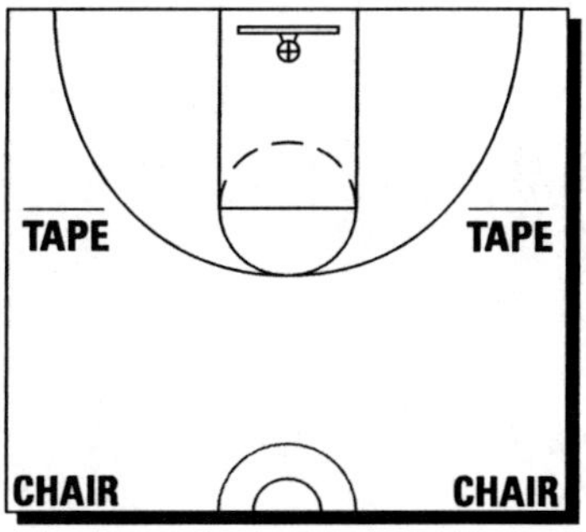

The wings must run wide. We put chairs on the floor. They would have to make the cut around the tape. The 3-point shooter usually runs on the left side. She can stop at the line.

Shot Selection: How are you going to determine who is going to shoot the ball the most? Whom do you want to shoot the ball the most? We have simple rules. If you shoot 50%, you can shoot from wherever you want. Of our first seven players, five shot 50% or better, two shot 48%. We have good shot selection. They know their abilities. But, you must establish rules for your players. I don't tell them their role. The players tell me their role by what they can do. I don't stifle their creativity. What can they do? I had a player whom I wouldn't let shoot outside of 5' from the basket. She only shot 52% from the line. And, she wants to shoot free throw jumpers with someone in her face. You tell me what your role is, and you need stats to back it up. If you want to be a shooter, shoot an extra 100 a day and tell me how many you made. If you don't want to put in the extra time to get better, then you've got to match her skills with her shot selection.

Passing: How are you turning the ball over? We didn't turn it over on the break. We turned it over every possible way. So, we can't eliminate one part of our game and eliminate our turnovers. How did you turn it over?

DIAGRAM 5-15.

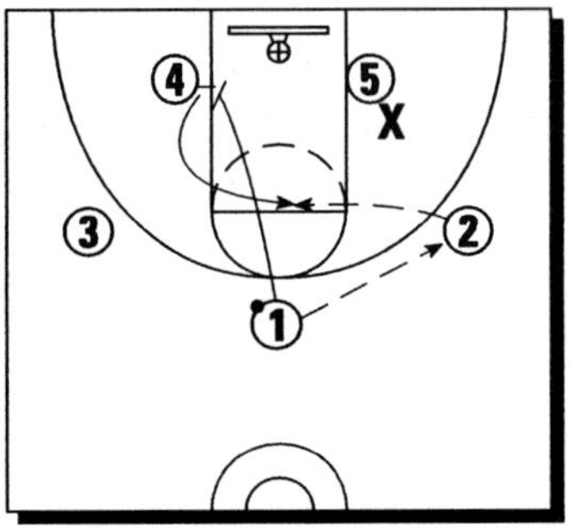

Back to the break. 2 has the ball. Now what? I am a firm believer that post defense is the toughest thing to teach. If you are a good offensive player, you will be open on the first pass or the second one. The obvious way is 1-2-5 with 2 making the bounce pass to the post. We don't lob from the wing to the post. If 5 is fronted, the ball should be reversed to the top. 1 sets the diagonal screen, and 4 comes high to bring the defense out. On the pass from 2 to 4, 5 pins the defense. So, 1-2-4-5. If the defense fights over the top and 5 wants a lob, 5 points high.

DIAGRAM 5-16.

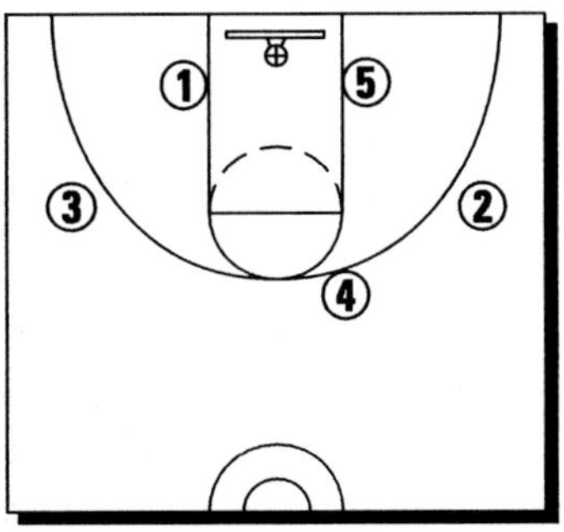

This is our *"power game"* set.

Question: When you *"run out of the net,"* what do you do against pressure?

Answer: Running after a made field goal helps us to get the ball in. When you get the ball in quickly, you can often go long. They tried to take the 1-to-2 pass away. Since I don't like to have a different press offense for a man and zone, etc., we do the same thing, and then we change 5. She screens and comes back to the ball. Teaching points to the pass to 5. We have one basic rule. You cannot be the post if you are not going to the free-throw line. You must get below the line. You must read the defense and make the bounce pass away from the defense.

DIAGRAM 5-17.

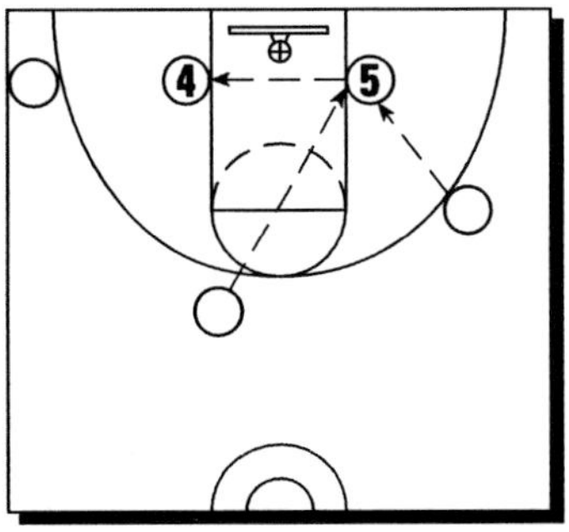

5 looks for 4 cutting, and then looks opposite. If you have a post player who cannot make a layup, make her a passer. Look opposite for the 3-point shot.

DIAGRAM 5-18.

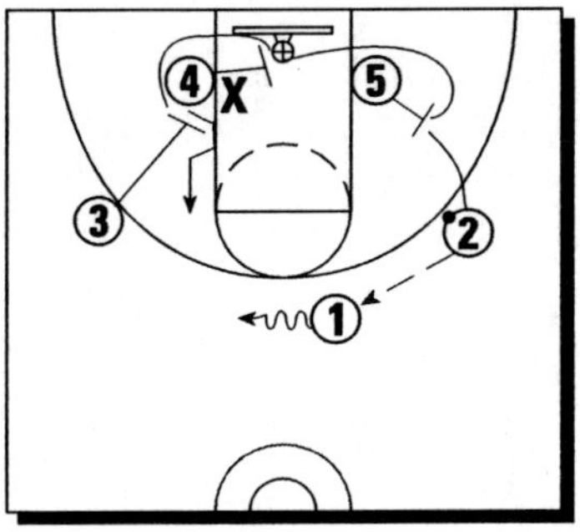

If you have a good perimeter game, do this. If you set a good screen, you will get a good shot. If the defense follows, 2 curls.

DIAGRAM 5-19.

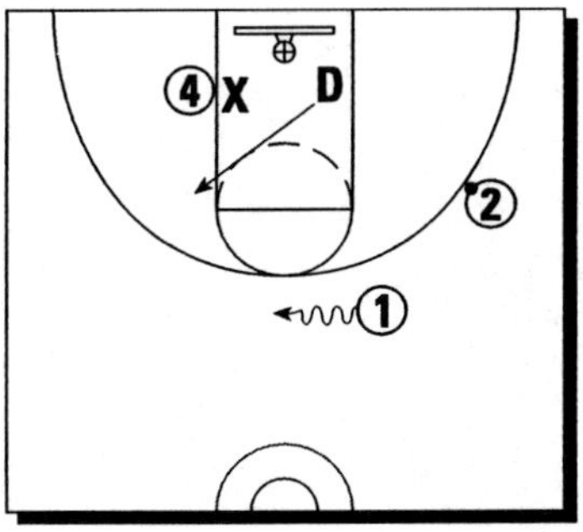

If the defense goes over the top, 2 fades to corner. The point guard must read the defense and move the ball into position without getting in the way of 2. Usually, the defense will if you can't rebound, you must get very good shots. You must also work on rebounding the 3-point shots. You must also determine your *philosophy.* Do you want to be Loyola Marymount or Princeton? Do you want to be deliberate or run and shoot every seven seconds? Not all players like this, for example, most big people don't. They rebound and get to half-court, and the guards are coming back from the shot. Soon, they stop rebounding. The question with this is "how much control do you want to have?" I like to have control. I want to run, but I also want good percentage shots. You must look at your defensive philosophy too. I think that you must go all out in both directions or not at all. I don't think that you can press and then play deliberate offense.

About *conditioning.* Some teams use the track during the actual season. They run 200s and 400s twice a week. We use the track before the season. One of our drills is the 6-4-6. Start on the baseline. Run six sprints up and run back twice. Then, backpedal four times, then run six again. We do this in 1 minute and 50 seconds.

DIAGRAM 5-20.

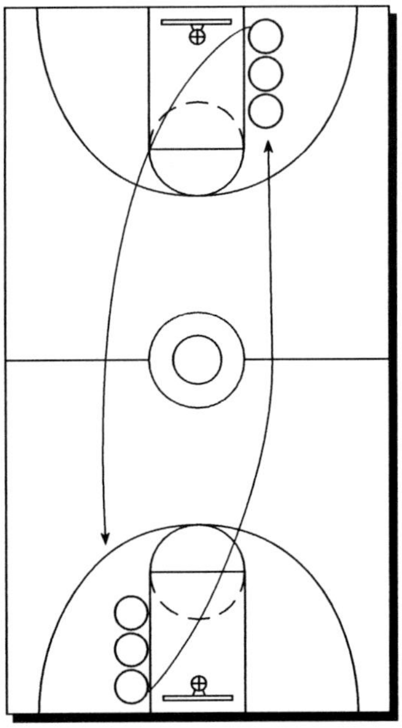

We do a two-minute tap drill. You can also make them run with their hands in the air. Put the ball on the backboard and change lines. Don't let the ball hit the floor. We also run 16 sidelines across court in a minute. We put 10 or 15 seconds on the clock and play a game. You must shoot in 10 seconds.

Question: What passing drills do you do?

Answer: First, teach the fundamentals, use a square, and show them what you want. We do a lot of double-team passing drills, feeding the post 2/2. We practice the bounce pass. We do player in the middle, an offensive post with a guard feeder. The defensive player drops into the middle when the post has the ball, and comes back out to guard the perimeter player when the ball goes back out. Do this for 25 seconds.

Where do you get a lot of your ideas? Clinics are one source. I watched the men's team play, saw a good zone offense, changed it a little, and put it in. When we play against someone who has an out-of-bounds play that gives us trouble, we will be running it next week.

DIAGRAM 5-21.

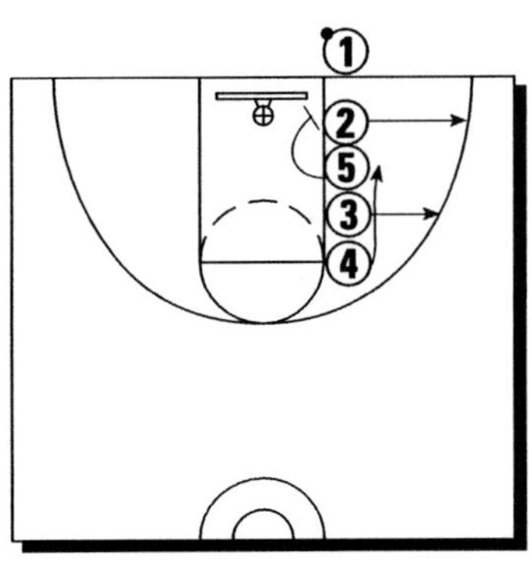

Inbounds play vs zone. Any kind of overload vs. a zone gives it trouble. 2 is a good shooter. 5 must make the center guard her. 5 pins in the lane. 3 goes to 3-point line. 4 steps down the lane.

DIAGRAM 5-22.

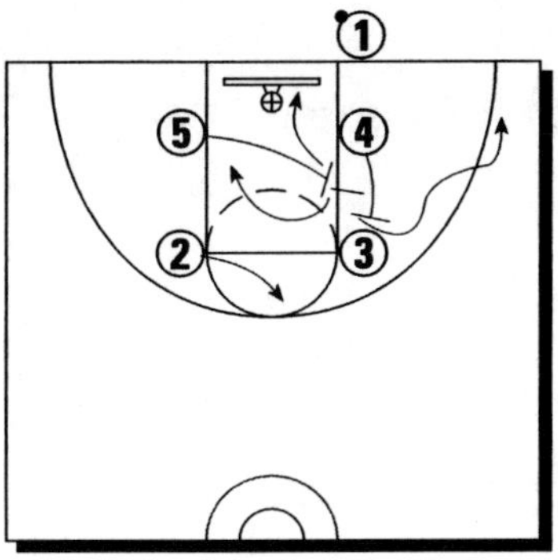

Box. Screen the screener. You must get the proper angle. 4 screens for 3 who goes to the 3-point area. 5 screens for 4 who screens the screener. 5 rolls to basket. 2 plays defense.

Question: How do you attack the half-court trap?

Answer: With a 2-1-2.

DIAGRAM 5-23.

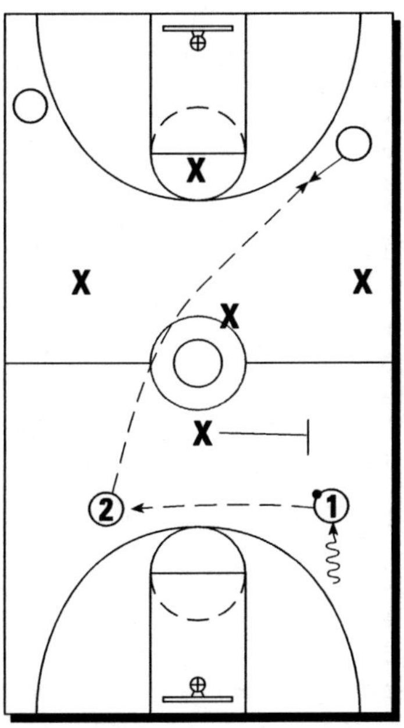

Where are they going to trap? Do they wait until they go over half-court or do they trap you earlier? 1 dribbles until the trap starts to form and passes across to 2, who then makes the baseball pass. The defense must run from the free-throw line to the corner before 1 makes the pass. 2 can also make the pass to the girl in the middle. Sometimes, we put a guard in the middle, someone who can handle the ball. Then, we take it to the basket.

DIAGRAM 5-24.

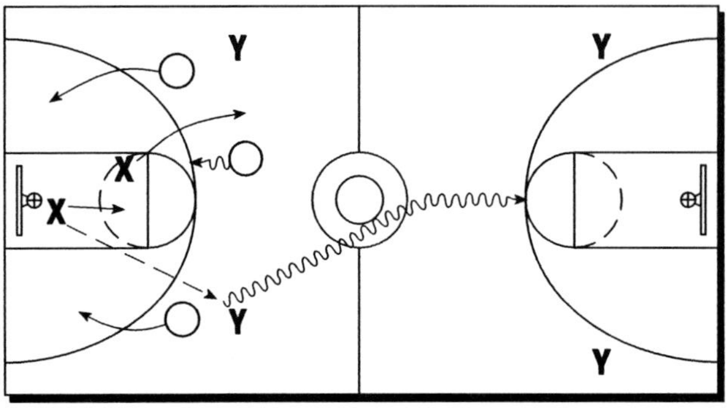

The 3-man break, a 3/2 on both ends.

1 Point Guard—must be intelligent, a good passer, make good decisions, unselfish, and willing to give up the ball.

#2 and #3—We have been using three guards, and they are interchangeable. Hopefully, one of them is a 3-point shooter. Our best player has been our #2 guard. She is very fast, gets down the floor quickly because she doesn't block out. So, we usually have her guard the point guard. Our point guard is a better rebounder anyway.

#4 and #5—also interchangeable. First one down goes to the ballside block. You can designate either to be the inbounder. We really use more than one. We designate certain players to NOT inbound the ball. If we have several inbounders in the game at the same time, whoever is closest inbounds the ball.

DIAGRAM 5-25.

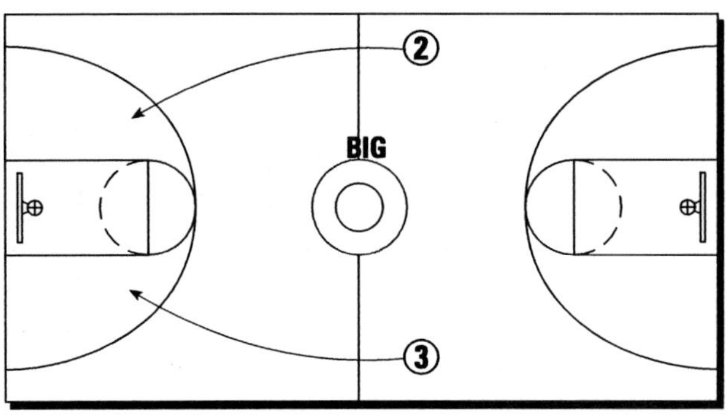

On the break, 2 and 3 are wide, with big people in the middle of the floor. We outlet to 2 or 3 if she is open. You can't get too predictable. Our only rule is that you can't throw it cross court. You must be on the left side of the floor to throw to 3, the right side to throw to 2. 2 was our best 1/1 player, and was allowed to go 1/1.

DIAGRAM 5-26.

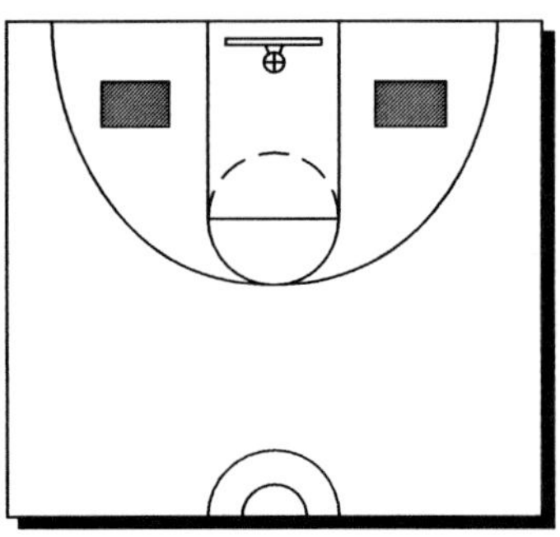

Don't allow your wings to drift. I tell my team, there is one shot I don't want, and it's this one.

CHAPTER 6

THE FAST BREAK

Jim O'Brien

I'd like to preface my remarks by telling you where I am coming from because it's important for you to understand what makes me tick, why I do the things I do. I am going to speak about the fast break, but I am also going to put in the 3-point shot throughout the fast break. We can go over how we get the 3-point shot in the half court also. I will cover special situations near the end of the game and how to get a 3-point shot at the end of the game.

I am absolutely passionate about the up-tempo game. I think it is a tremendous way to play, very exciting for players, great for recruiting. It emotionally turns on the players at any level.

I was an assistant coach at various schools before I became the head coach at Wheeling Jesuit College, a small NAIA school. While I was there, we ran some years, we pressed some years, but we never did them both together. I felt players had to rest sometimes, and if you didn't provide that chance, they would find it themselves.

I then went to the Knicks with Rick Pitino and learned that there was a way that you could press and run and keep the pressure on your opponent for the entire game. Not only that, but the pressure enabled you to take advantage of the 3-pointer.

When I got the job at the University of Dayton, I inherited a program that had a very good coach. However, that coach had struggled for three straight years. He played a very low tempo game. During a press conference, I said that we were going to press, we were going to run, and we were going to shoot the 3-point shot. I had six seniors coming back who had not won during their time at Dayton.

I told the press that we were going to *run and shoot the 3*. The question asked was: "You mean after this team graduates?" I said we would do it now and was almost laughed out of the place. We did exactly as I had proclaimed. We won the championship of the league, and went to the NCAA and beat Illinois and then played Arkansas. We lost to them at the buzzer, 96-94.

I would suggest that by taking these same players out of a low-tempo style that we really energized them. This is a key concept and one that is often overlooked by coaches. It is important that players want to compete with a high-energy level. It is easier to motivate people when the team knows you are going to play ten or eleven people every game, that they are going to get a chance to shoot the ball, and that they are going to go up and down the court.

No matter what level you are coaching, during the summer, your players are going to shoot the 3-point shot on a regular basis ,whether it is your philosophy or not. Players want to shoot the 3; players want to run.

Defensively, we are pressing 100% of the time. You can't take what I am talking about offensively and forget that we press defensively. We want to stay in your face the entire game.

DIAGRAM 6-1.

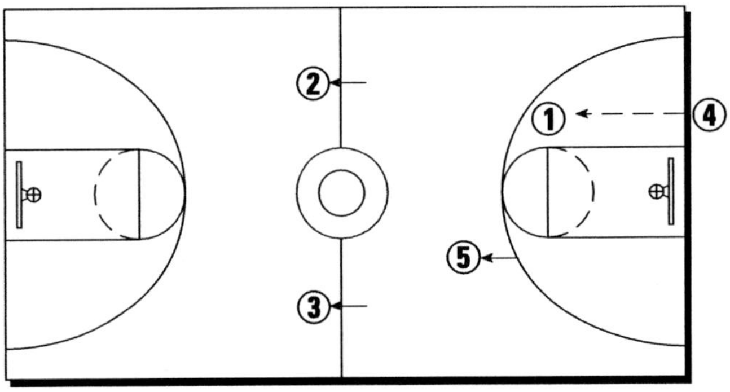

We run a *numbered break,* and we number in the traditional way; 1 is point guard, 2 and 3 were both small this year, 4 is the power forward and 5 is the center. This year, we only allowed 4 to take the ball out. 1 always got the ball. 2 went down the right, 3 down the left, and 5 streaked down the middle. You need a strong inside presence in order to be a strong 3-point shooting team. We were more effective in running the break after the made shot because we were more organized. 1 does not come below the foul line extended. If you get the ball in quickly, rarely will a press be quick enough to stop your inbounds pass.

DIAGRAM 6-2.

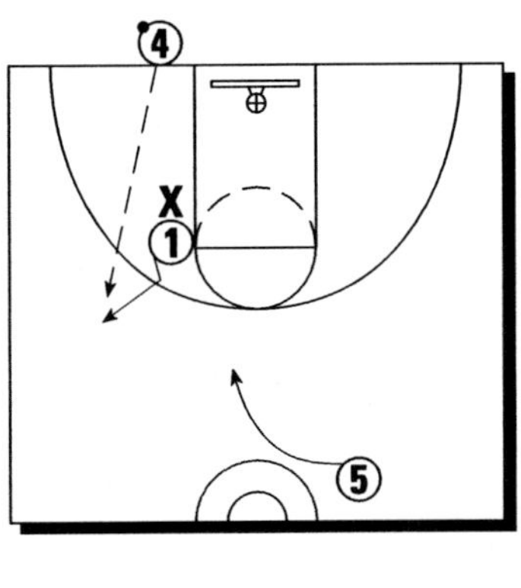

But if 1 is denied the ball by being fronted, 1 will *jab step* and go toward the mid-right lane, halfway between the sideline and the foul lane extended. We don't want him to make the angle pass over the defense to the outside shoulder of 1. When 5 gets to the center circle, he is looking over his shoulder.

DIAGRAM 6-3.

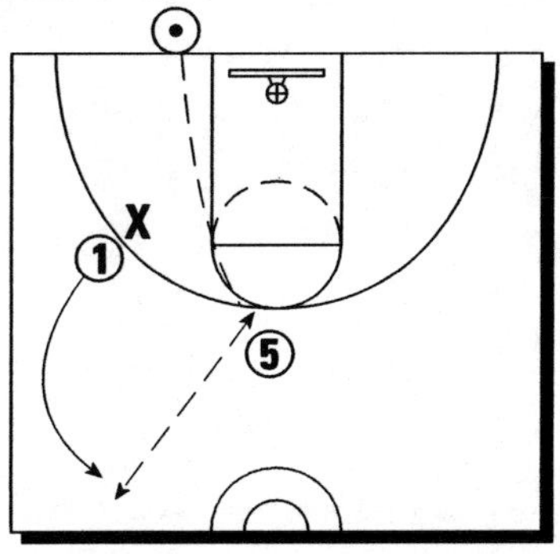

If 1 does not get the ball, 4 throws a high pass to 5 halfway between the center circle and the foul line. You must pick up the little things that make this go.

Footwork is so important. We want all of our people, when they start to sprint down the floor, to use the crossover step. We put all our players on the baseline and run them the length of the floor. You will be surprised how many players don't have their knees bent. You will also be surprised how many players false step (i.e., take a small step before they bring the other foot through).

If you can teach your players to stay in their stance, then, when they start to go to work on their crossover step, you are ahead of the game. 4 is taught to get to the rim with extended hands so he catches the ball as it comes out of the net. If he waits, you don't have a fast break.

Once we get the ball, we turn immediately, even before he gets out of bounds, he observes what is happening up court. We drill this. Where 1 catches the ball is dependent on the defense. If there is no press, we want 1 to catch the ball as close to half court as possible. We scout this. We want the ball advanced up the court as far as possible on the first pass.

Question: Do you have 4 throw a 2-handed pass or a baseball pass?
Answer: Whatever is comfortable for him. Some people just aren't comfortable with the baseball pass. But, the *pass must be quick.*

DIAGRAM 6-4.

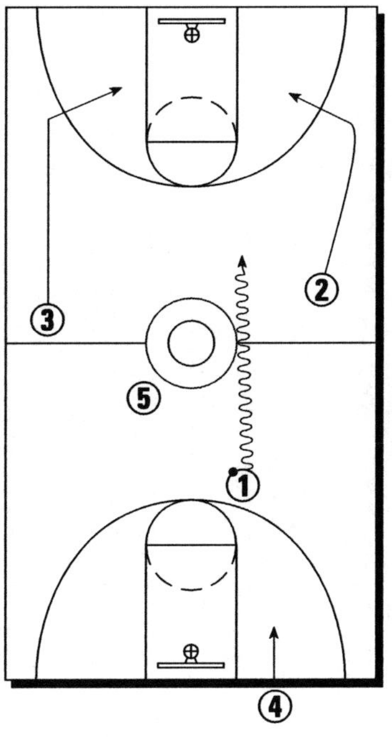

This is not a sideline fast break. We want the ball straight up toward the other elbow. One of the things we do every day is 5/0, and we want everyone on the team to get a shot. They make five trips down the court in 30 seconds or less. You really push the ball. If the shot is made, 4 takes it out. We have a *sequence.* The first time down, 4-to-1-to-2, and he shoots. Then, 4-to-1-to-3. Then, 1 shoots off the dribble. These are all 3-point shots.

DIAGRAM 6-5.

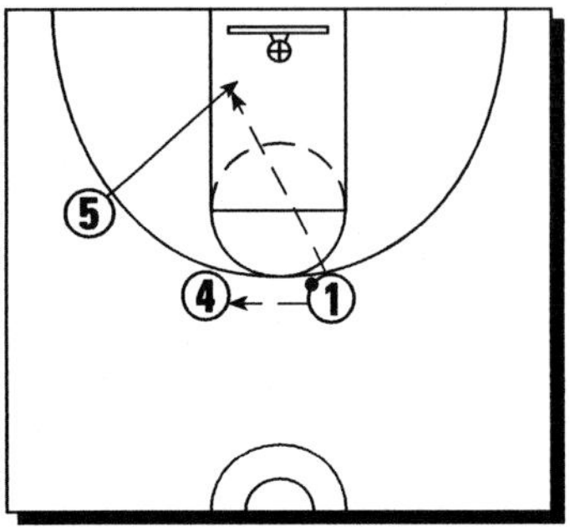

4-to-1-to-5 for a layup, and 4-to-1-to-4 for a 3-point shot. Early in the year, we want *speed instead of accuracy.* The shooting will come.

DIAGRAM 6-6.

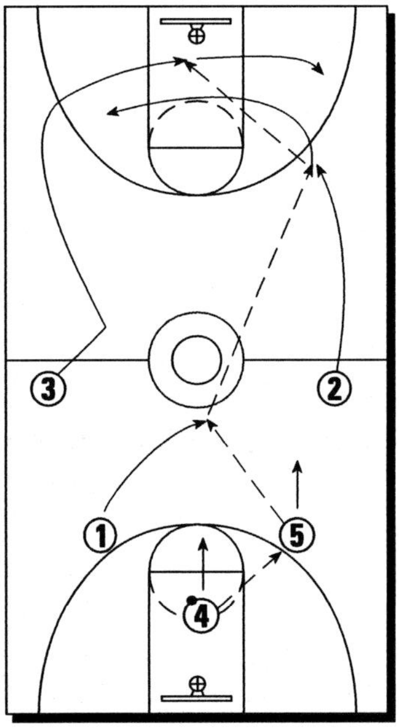

This is similar to the weave. 4-to-5-to-1-to-2-to-3 for a layup. 4 must sprint and catch the ball out of the net, take it out of bounds, and start again. 2 and 3, 1 and 5, exchange under and fill the lanes. We want 2 and 3 to be right on the sidelines. When we come down the court and we're not able to advance the ball in the initial break, 1 still has the ball.

DIAGRAM 6-7.

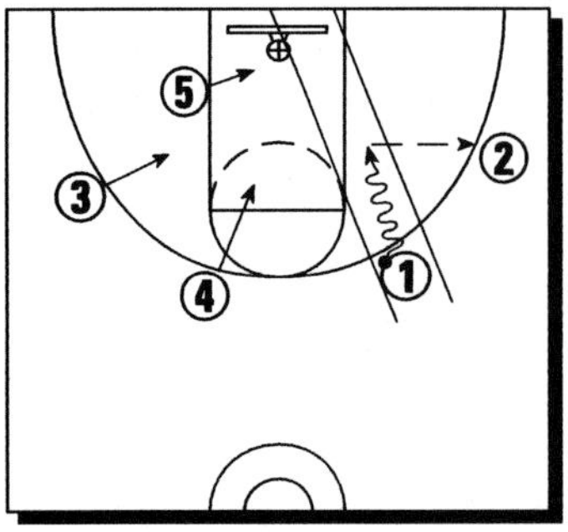

On our fast break, we do not fill the ballside low post when 1 has the ball. We want to keep a driving lane for 1. In my mind, everything starts with the point guard. I want the point guard to be as aggressive as possible. We want to attack and put the defense back on its heels. Then we can pass out for the 3-point shot, penetrate, draw the defense, and pass out for the 3. If 1's man backs off, 1 shoots the 3. We also have the 3,4, and 5 crashing the boards from the weakside.

DIAGRAM 6-8.

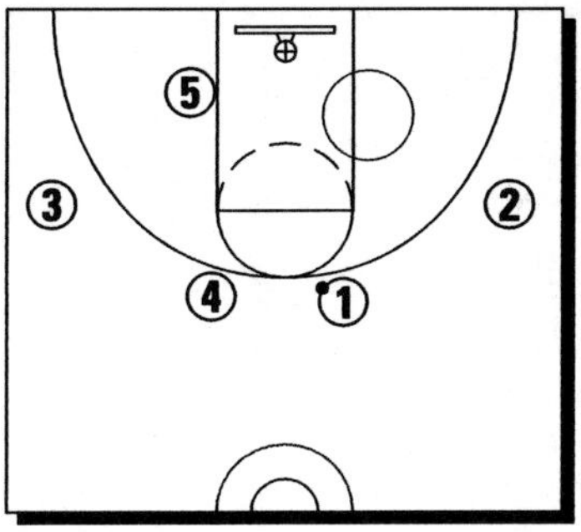

If there is one thing that we all will agree on, it is to get back and cover ballside. So, we put 5 on the other side. When we reverse the ball, 5 has a better chance to get it.

DIAGRAM 6-9.

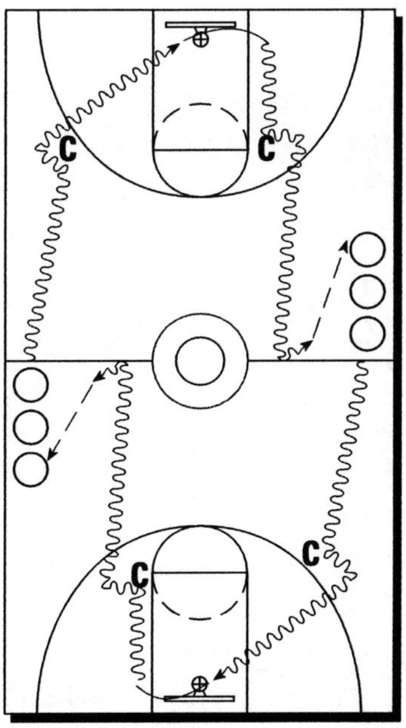

We want all of our people, large and small, to be able to attack the basket with either hand, full speed. This is the drill we use. Everybody has a ball. We have four coaches on the floor. Each player starts with the *speed dribble* to where the hash mark used to be. He attacks the defensive player by the coach and blows by with his left hand and goes to the basket for a layup, planting the foot above the box to get a good 45-degree angle off the glass. They get their own rebound, and attack the other coach, going by shoulder-to-shoulder at full speed to half court. They then go to the end of the other line. When you go by the defense, you must go by shoulder-to-shoulder and go in a straight line to the basket. We use the *speed dribble, the hesitation dribble, the in-out dribble, and the crossover dribble.* The next day, we will do it right-handed.

CHAPTER 7

FUNDAMENTALS FOR THE FAST BREAK

JOHNNY ORR

CONDITIONING DRILLS FOR THE FAST BREAK

DIAGRAM 7-1. 4-MAN CONVERSION

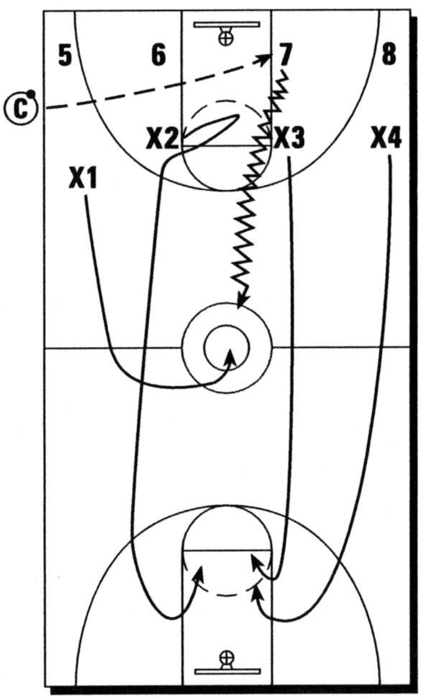

The coach throws the ball to 5, 6, 7, or 8. Now 1, 2, 3, or 4 cannot guard the man directly in front of them — they have to pick up someone else. 7 gets the ball from the coach. As soon as the ball is thrown in, 2, 3, and 4 all take off and drop back — we tell them get in the paint. Let's say 1 takes 7. We want 1 to pick up 7 as quickly as he can and stop him immediately. 2, 3, and 4 get to the point, and then they go and find their men as quickly as they can. If 5, 6, 7, and 8 get an offensive advantage (e.g., 1-on-1, 3-on-2), they go ahead and score, so they go.

If 1 has picked up 7 and everybody else is back, we tell 5, 6, 7, and 8 they must make three or five passes before they can take a shot. They can move anywhere they want, but we just don't let them come down and shoot the ball right away. Then, we turn around and come back. The same guys, 1, 2, 3, and 4, are on defense, and 5, 6, 7, and 8 are on offense. After they come back down, the defensive group rotates off the court, and 5, 6, 7 and 8 go on defense, and a new offensive group comes on.

Conversion is as important as anything in the game — you have to get back to protect against the easy basket. We also do 3-lane running; we run the lines; and we also run straight down.

DIAGRAM 7-2. STRAIGHT DOWN

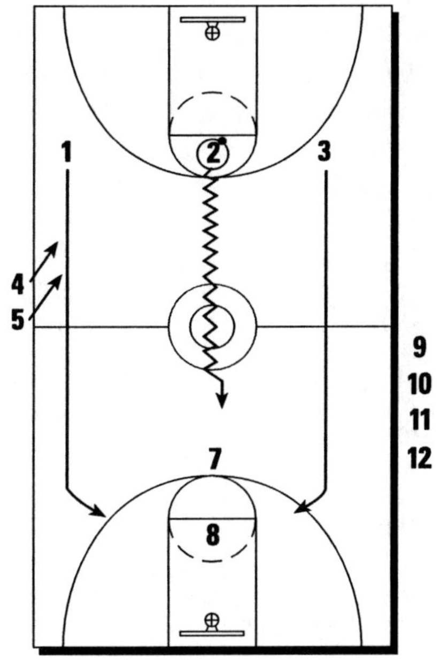

1, 2, 3, 4, 5, and 6 are one group. 7, 8, 9, 10, 11, and 12 are another. We start out with 1, 2, and 3 with the ball and 4 and 5 stay back for defense. At the other end, 7 and 8 are on defense, and 9, 10, 11 and 12 are on the side. Each group is in different color jerseys, and they rotate off the court to the same side each time. At this point, 1, 2, and 3 bring the ball down. We used to tell the dribbler to bring the ball all the way down, but now we say if a man ahead of you is open, give it to him and then go. 7 has to stop the ball. 8 takes the first pass, and 8 *must not* allow his man to shoot. 7 has to drop quickly to the basket or else 8's man will throw the ball across. As soon as the dribbler comes down, 9 (out of bounds at half-court) sprints to the circle and then gets back to pick up 2. We call this "3-man continuous."

DIAGRAM 7-3. 3-MAN CONTINUOUS

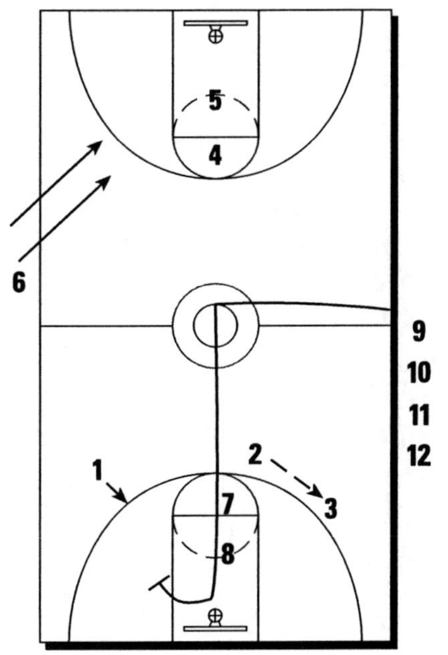

If the offense has 3-on-2, they have a fast break — that's what we're teaching. They can get it without fumbles or interceptions.

But, if the defense hustles, they can get back and stop the break, because even in college, you'd be amazed how many times there is a fumble or something goes wrong. So if the defense *hustles back,* they can get the job done. If there has been no shot by 1, 2, or 3 and the defense now has 9 back, it's 3-on-3. We can now make 1, 2 and 3 pass the ball five times, or until they get a lay-up. On the shot, all six go for the ball, the defense blocks out, and the offense crashes and goes and gets it!

DIAGRAM 7-4.

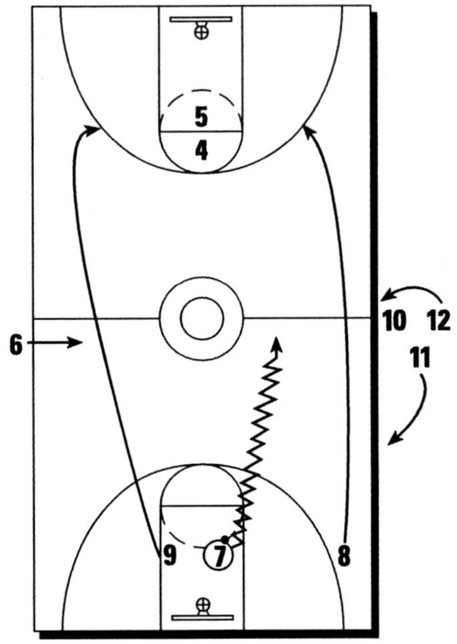

We want the offense to be aggressive going to the boards. If the defense gets it, the offense lets them go the other way. If 1, 2, or 3 get the rebound, they try to put it back in again. If the defense (7, 8, 9) get it, they break the other way against 4 and 5 (Diagram 7-4) who are already back on defense. 6 is out of bounds at mid-court waiting to enter to help 4 and 5 just as 9 did with 7 and 8. Sometimes, we keep score. The coach "refs" and we may play to 7 or 10 baskets. It's a conditioning drill, it's ballhandling, and it's adjustment too. As 7, 8, and 9 break, 10 and 11 go to defense, and 12 waits at mid-court. It's continuous. It's an offensive rebounding drill too.

DIAGRAM 7-5. THREE-MAN-STRAIGHT DOWN

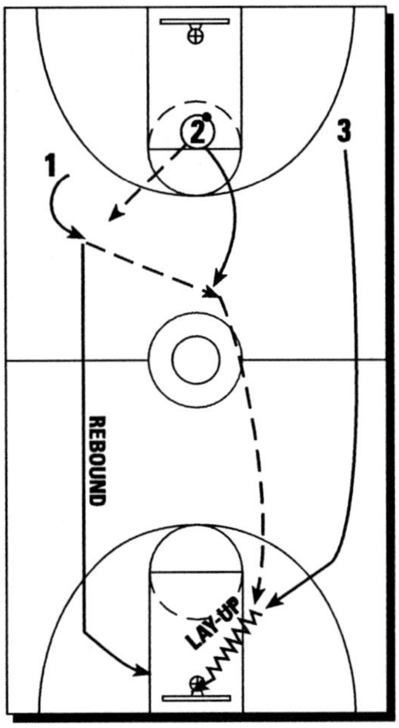

2 passes to 1 and moves, 1 return passes to 2. As we start, 3 goes. 2 passes down to 3 so that 3 catches it on the run and lays it in the basket. As soon as 1 passes to 2, 1 is gone. He's going after the rebound. 2, who passed to 3, is now gone. He sprints to touch the endline. As soon as 2 touches the endline, he turns and is on his way back.

DIAGRAM 7-6.

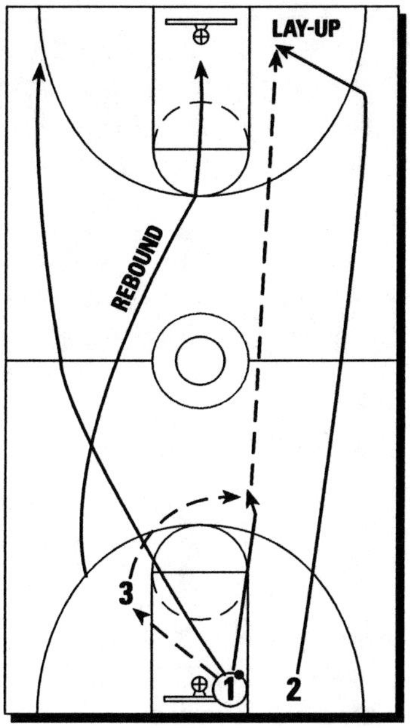

1 gets the rebound, passes to 3 who moves over and 3 passes it back to 1. 1 throws the long pass to 2 for a lay-up, while 3 goes for the rebound and 1 sprints to touch the endline.

DIAGRAM 7-7.

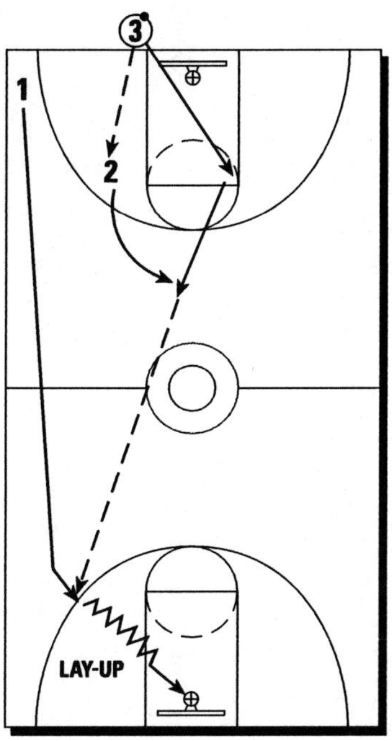

Then, they come back. When your kids can do this without putting the ball on the floor, you are "running." You will find out who can run, who can pass, and who can't. If you go *down and back* three times, they will get two lay-ups each, they will have played all three positions, and they will be tired.

DIAGRAM 7-8. SHELL DRILL

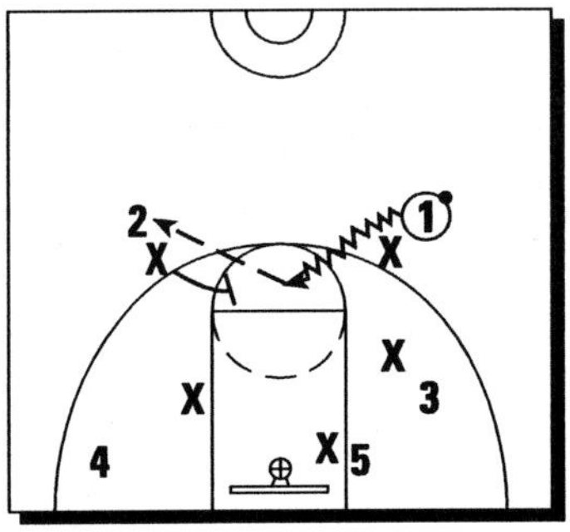

We use this drill all the time because everything that can be used against us, offensively or defensively, can be covered with this set. For example, if the dribbler penetrates, we're working on help and recover. We cover the block out by moving the ball around and then taking a shot. The coaches look for good block-out coverage.

DIAGRAM 7-9.

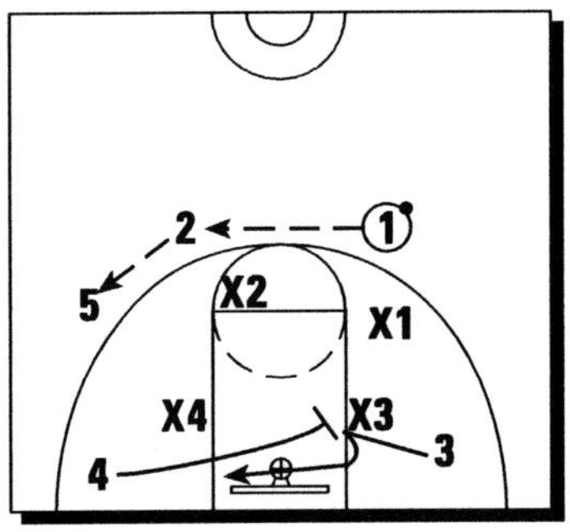

We get the outlet pass and get ready to run the break. We work against "screen across." We want 4 to come across on a high move, and we force 3 to go low every time. The screener's man (X-4) stays until the guy being screened (X-3) gets him. We never worry about the screener. X-1 will go with 1 part way and come back, until X-3 can get in between his teammate (X-1) and 1 can get up to pick up 3. We do the same on a "back screen." If your man goes up to set a back screen, the defense does not go with him—let him go. Now, "help" and then go to your man (recover); we play man-to-man, and we do not shift men because we get people psyched up to cover certain people.

DIAGRAM 7-10.

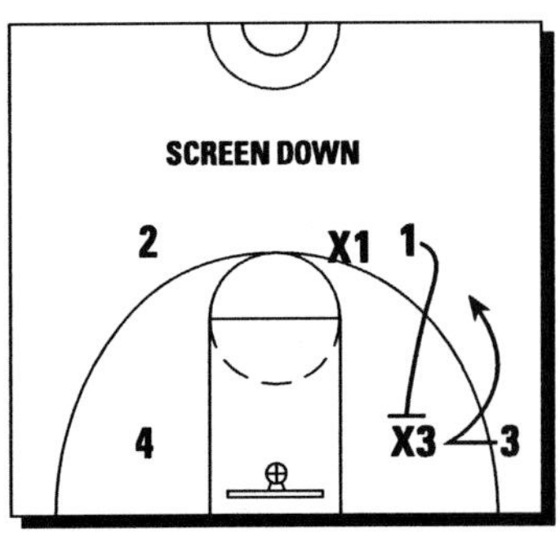

DIAGRAM 7-11. PENETRATE THE PRESS

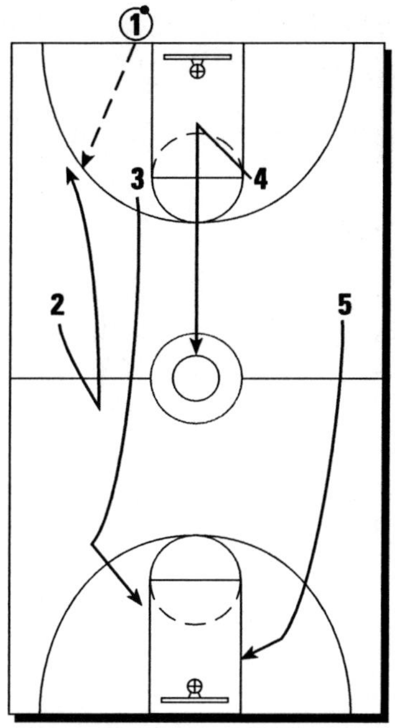

Diagrams 7-11 to 7-14 illustrate how we penetrate the press, whether it's man-to-man, 2-2-1, 1-2-2, or 1-3-1. If it's a stationary throw-in, then your guys have to get active. We set 2 as high as the hash mark. 2 goes down and back, and we'd like to enter it to him at this point. The press wants you to get it down below the foul line extended so they can trap you. 1 hits 2, and 4 goes. If 4 is free, 2 hits 4. 3 has come back toward 1. 3 then goes, so we try to get the ball to 4 with 3 and 5 going.

DIAGRAM 7-12.

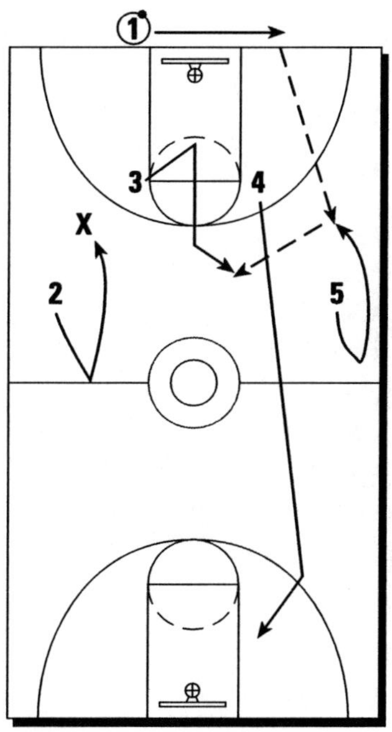

We're off and running. 1 runs to the other side, and 5 does what 2 did. 1 hits 5, and we look for 3 cutting. We'd like to get the ball down to 4 because if we can get it to him (1-on-1), he'll score most of the time — particularly if the defense puts a big guy back there.

DIAGRAM 7-13.

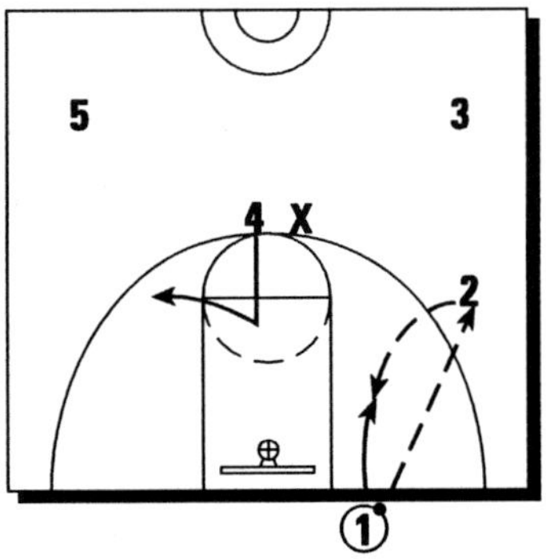

1 couldn't pass to 2 down the sideline, and now 2 has to come back closer. 1 passes to 2, and 1 steps in bounds. 2 passes back to 1. Before he does that, 2 looks to 4. But as a last resort, 2 gives it back to 1. 3 has moved down his right side. You saw this in Syracuse vs. Providence. The defense went man-to-man. The ball came into here, and they threw it down deep for an easy lay-up. That will happen to you. If you play man-to-man against us, we have 3 screen across on 4 who comes, and 3 opens to the ball.

DIAGRAM 7-14.

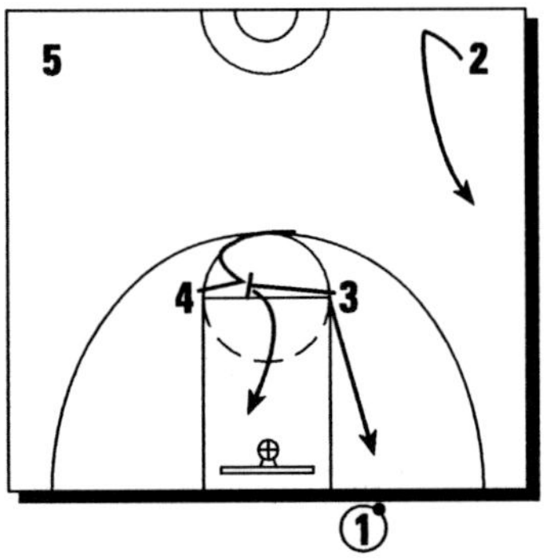

2 is still making his charge down and back—we'd like to get it to him first.

VERSUS HALF-COURT TRAPS

Any time it's a 1/2 court trap, we go to a high 2-3 alignment. Our rule is this: The guard with the ball always comes up the sideline (Diagram 7-15). He knows if he is going to be trapped, exactly who is going to trap him. As a result, he has no worries. He knows where the trap will be and by whom. The other guard (g) will trail G. So, if G does not cross the half-court line, he will whip the ball back to g, who will bring it to the left side as quickly as he can and G will move over to a trailer position. We take our best man and play him at the 3 position, and 4 and 5 are over to the side up high. Any time the defense leaves 3 alone, we want to get the ball to him. He immediately goes to the basket, with 4 and 5 also going hard. Our 3 has no restrictions as to where he can go to get the ball in that middle area, and when 3 gets it, the first thing he does is *turn and face them.*

DIAGRAM 7-15.

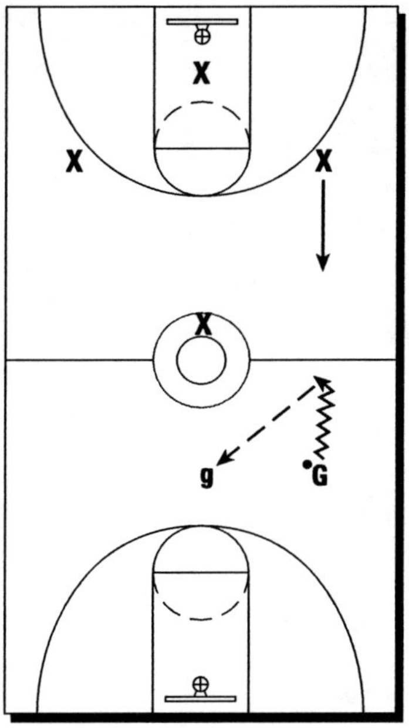

DIAGRAM 7-16.

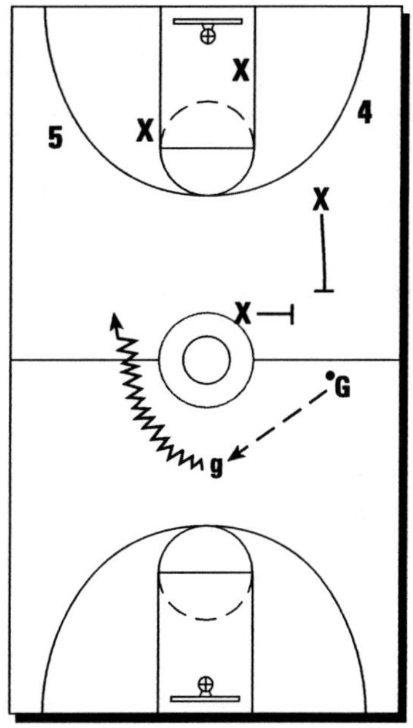

DIAGRAM 7-17.

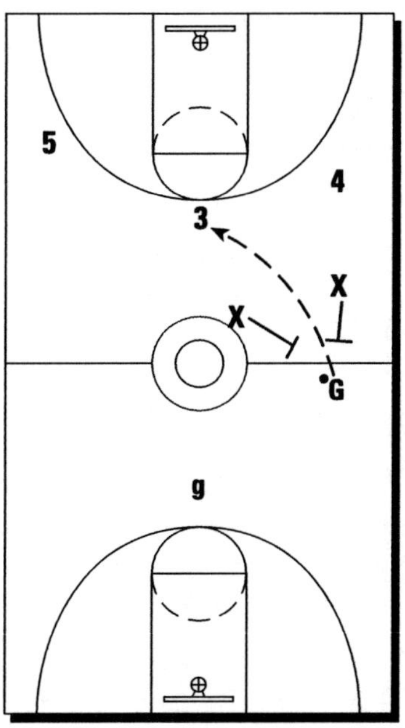

4 and 5 take off and go.

DIAGRAM 7-18.

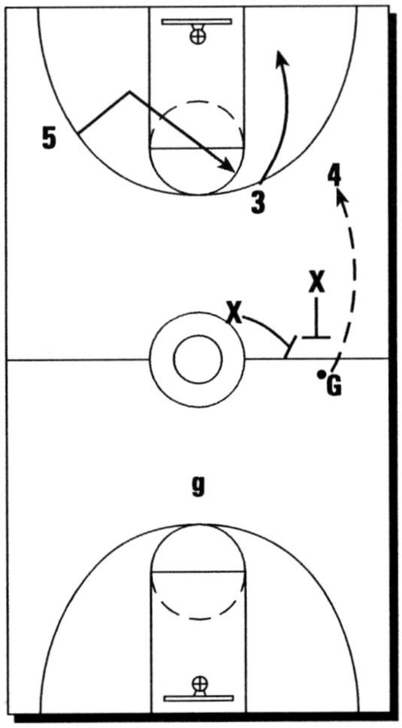

If G throws up the sideline to 4, then 3 rolls low, and we bring 5 high. If G has thrown to 5 on the other side, 3 rolls low, and 4 comes high. The decision is whether G comes across that half-court line or not. If he does well, tell him not to cross over and stop. He should not pick up his dribble; he stops, he's dead.

CHAPTER 8

TEACHING THE FAST BREAK

Tom Penders

During my career, I have had to coach every conceivable way. I can't emphasize enough that you must be able to adjust to your talent. You must coach your talent and develop an offense that your team can handle. You will be successful as long as you are adaptable to your talent. Here are some things that I have done in the last four years. We have gone to a running style. We run a very low-risk, quick-hitting, sound fundamental offense.

We run after a *made* basket. We think you get better fast-break opportunities and better shots then than after a miss becaus you can put people in places and positions that you want. Any time we get the ball after a dead ball, we are going to try to score in the next 10 seconds. I think that you get better opportunities in the first ten seconds than later. Fast-break basketball can be successful no matter how slow your teams are.

DIAGRAM 8-1.

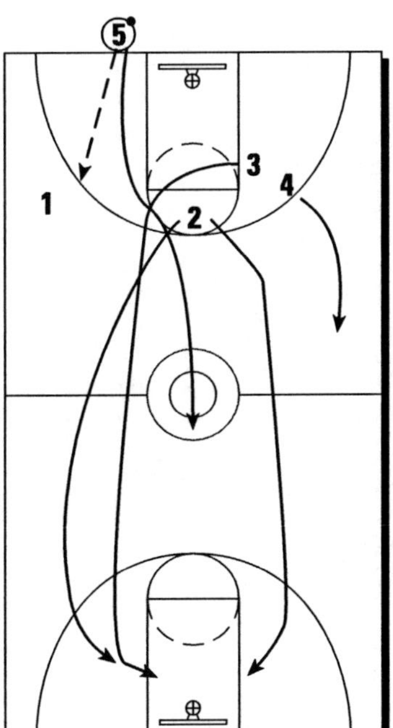

We number our break the usual way. 5 is the outlet man, the center. We want to get it out on the *right-hand side.* We take the ball up the sideline. 1 is on the *sideline* with his back to the sideline. He can see the whole floor before he dribbles. 1 never goes back to get the outlet pass, he stays between the foul line and the top of the circle. 4 is the secondary outlet, the power forward. He is below the foul line and inside the 3-point line away from outlet side. 3 releases to block on the ballside. 2, the other guard, goes on the fly pattern to either side in the 3-point shooting position.

DIAGRAM 8-2.

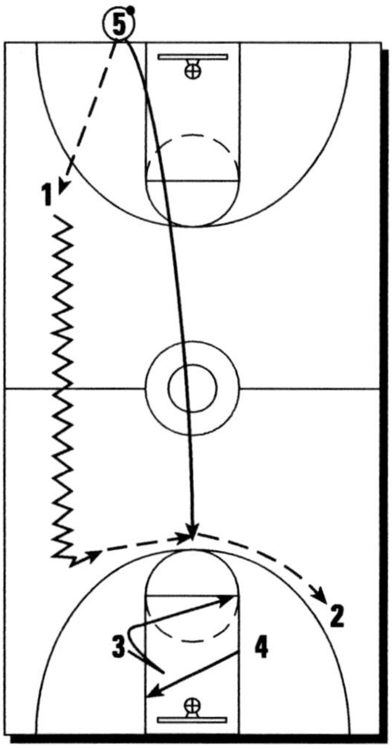

As soon as 4 sees the successful pass to 1, he sprints to the opposite block from 3. 1 gets the ball up the floor — the path of least resistance. We do not want the ball in the *middle.* We don't want him stopping at the *head of the key.* 5 trails. 1 to 5 to 2 for the 3-point shot. We took 683 3-point shots this year, shooting about 38%. Most came off of transition, for example, 5 screens down for 3 after passing to 2.

DIAGRAM 8-3.

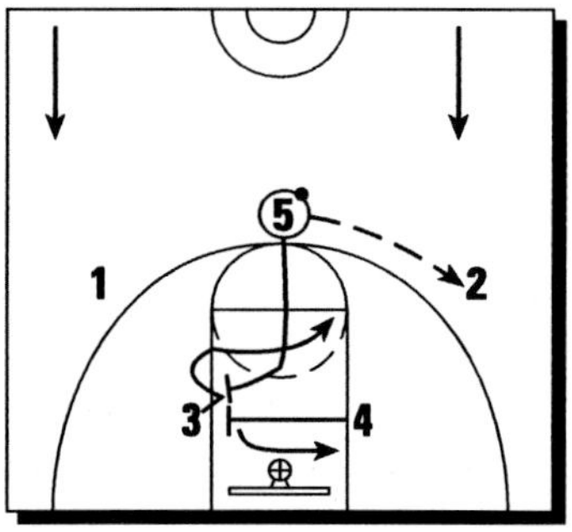

If we are running the flex series, 5 screens away for 3, 4 screens, and 2 looks for 5 on the block.

DIAGRAM 8-4.

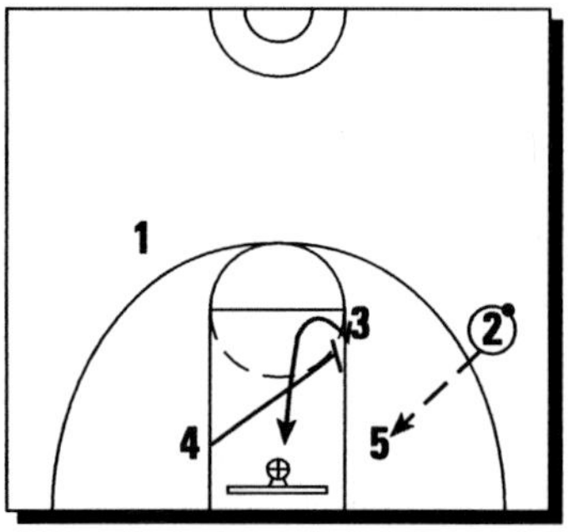

When the ball is thrown inside, the opposite block man always back-screens 4, who screens for 3.

DIAGRAM 8-5.

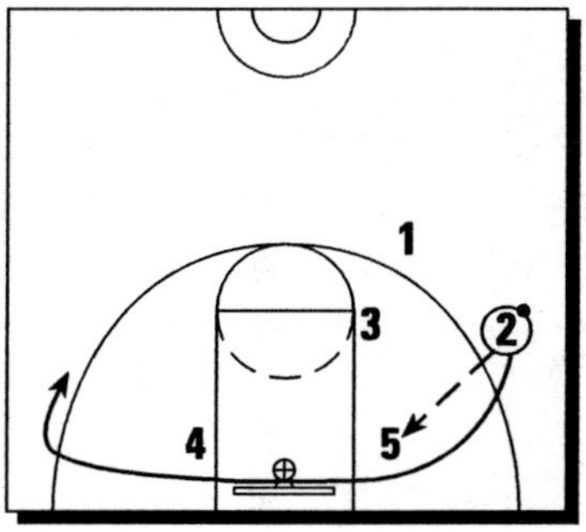

If 1 and 2 are on the same side, the ball should be passed into 5. 2 can cut through hard and be replaced by 1.

DIAGRAM 8-6.

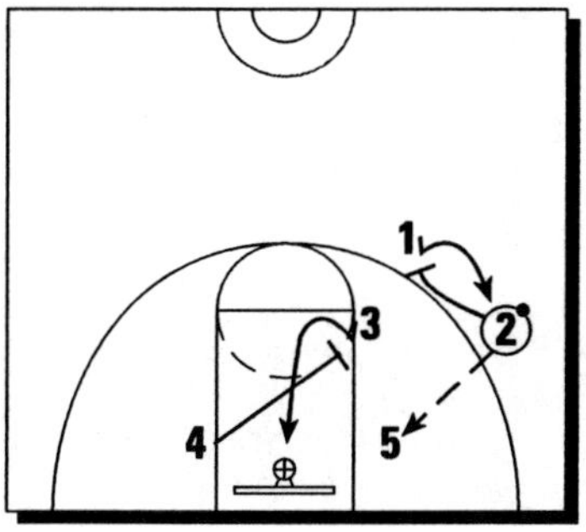

Another option that can be run is to have 2 pass into 5 and back-screen for 1, as 2 back-screens for 3.

DIAGRAM 8-7.

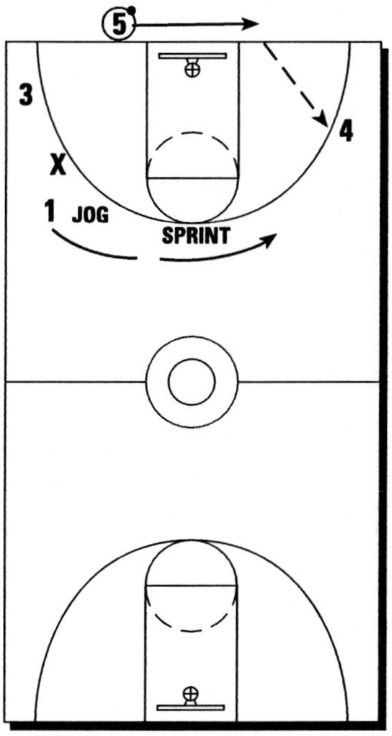

If teams try to *deny* the outlet pass to 1, 5 runs away from 1 and outlets to 4. 1 jogs until the pass is made to 4. Then, 1 *breaks hard* toward 4 for the ball. 2 starts down the floor and will hook into the middle if 1 and 4 cannot receive the pass.

DIAGRAM 8-8.

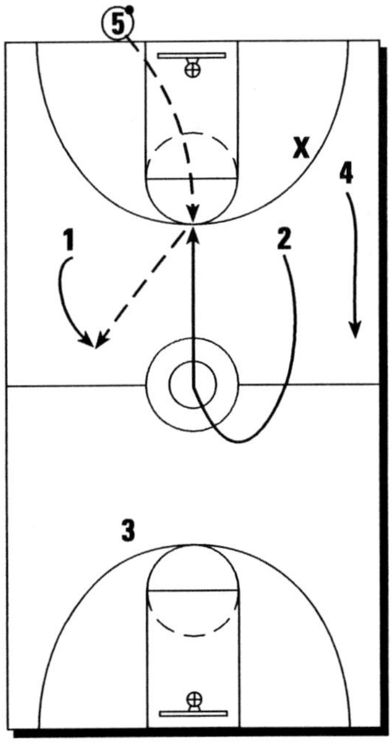

4 starts down the floor on the side. 1 also stays on the side so that 2 has room to receive the pass from 5 (5-to-2-to-1). 3 is down the floor.

DIAGRAM 8-9.

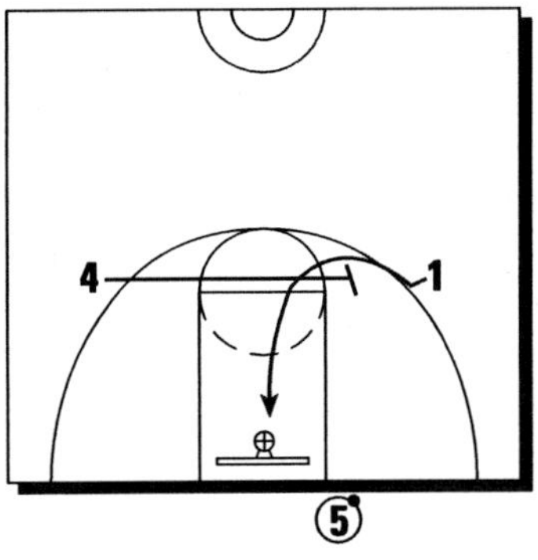

If you don't like this situation, 4 comes and screens for 1.

DIAGRAM 8-10.

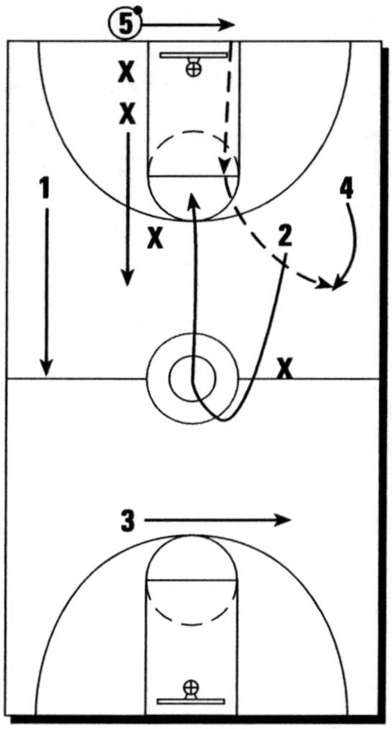

Against a press, we will still want to run and look to score. This is the *press offense* from the same basic set. 5 outlets. 1 and 4 are *decoys.* 1 breaks up the side and will take the defensive man with you. Same for 4. 2 hooks back for the pass (5-2-4-3). 3 goes to the ballside. 5 goes to the opposite side. We do not ask the 1 guard to break the press.

DIAGRAM 8-11.

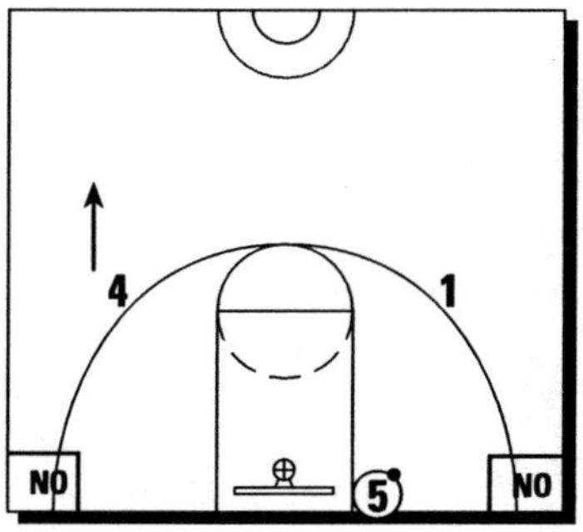

We do not allow our players to go into these areas to get the first pass. We don't come back for the ball. We press to make teams run and to play at our tempo. If you are being pressed a lot, get it in quickly and go, even if you don't shoot quickly at the other end.

DIAGRAM 8-12. VS. A 2-2-1 PRESS

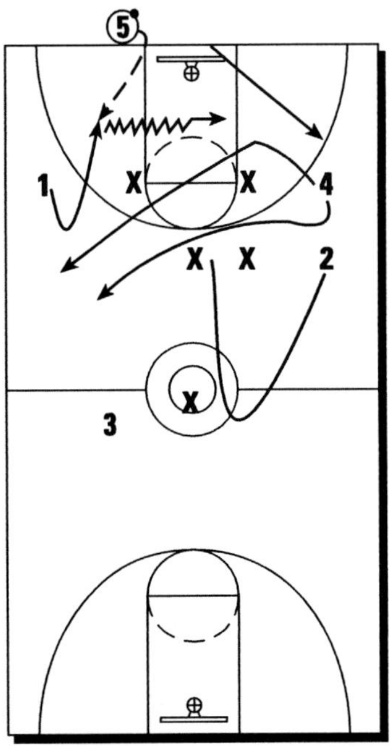

No one is on the ball. The first pass is thrown 5 to 1. 1 can *come back to the ball* if there is no defense on the ball. 2 *hooks* back behind the second line of defense. 3 is on the ballside. 1 dribbles to the center. 4 goes through the middle, preferably in front of the man, and then splits the difference between the two defenders. 5 does the same thing on the other side.

DIAGRAM 8-13.

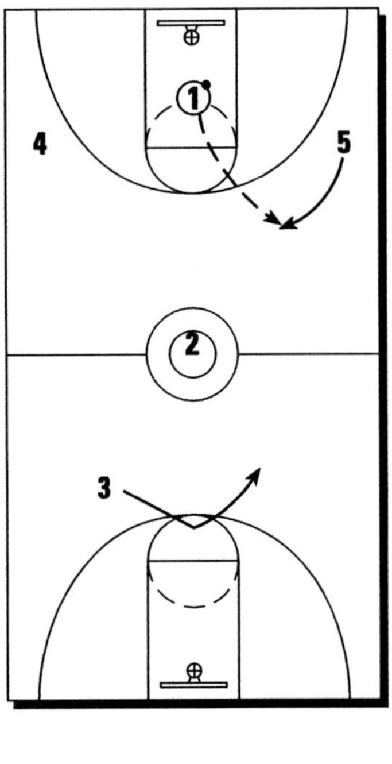

1 to 5, 1 to 4, 1 to 2. 3 goes to the ballside.

DIAGRAM 8-14. VS. 1-3-1 HALF-COURT TRAP

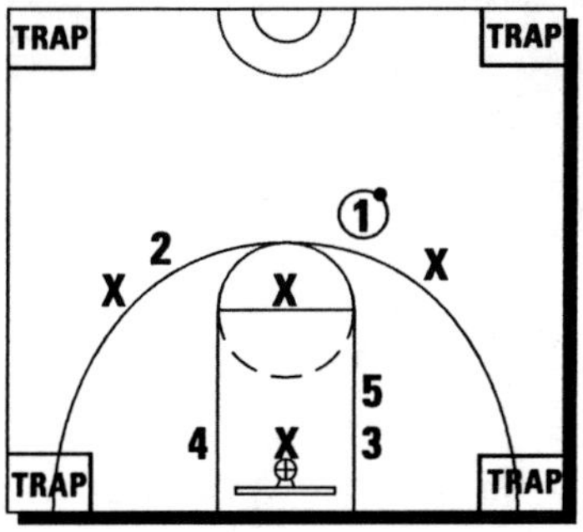

We want to score and score in a hurry. 3 is a decent shooter. If 1 has the ball, the opposite defensive wing *covers back.* Usually, the back man will trap with a wing. The middle man covers the low post, and the point man will take the high post when the trap is on.

DIAGRAM 8-15.

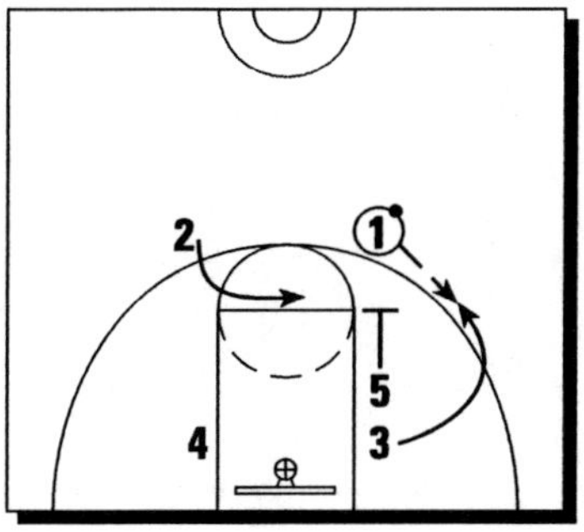

1 and 2 pass the ball back and forth a few times. Nothing starts until 2 drives to the elbow. 3 *pops out* on the baseline. 1 passes directly to 3 after dribbling at the wing. As the pass is being made, 5 backscreens the high-post defender, usually the middle man.

DIAGRAM 8-16.

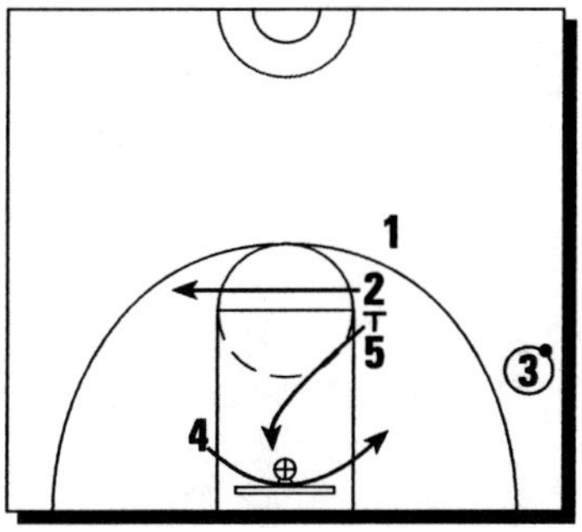

The ball is in the corner. 4 replaces, beating the weakside wing man to the spot. 2 sprints away to the wing spot. 3 to 4 or skip-pass to 2. 5 rolls to the block on the off-side.

DIAGRAM 8-17.

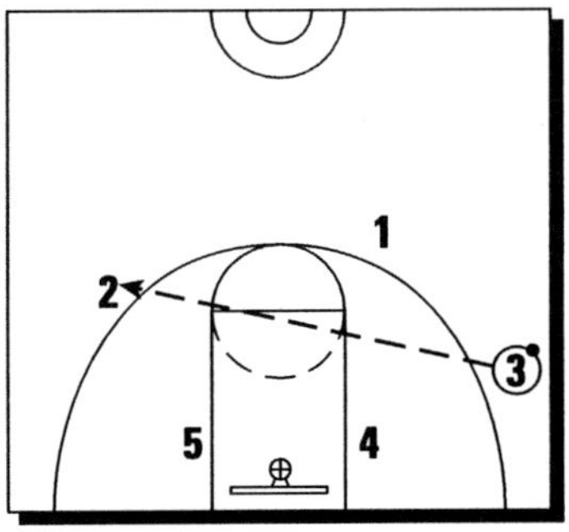

2 can shoot or pass to 5 for a layup.

DIAGRAM 8-18.

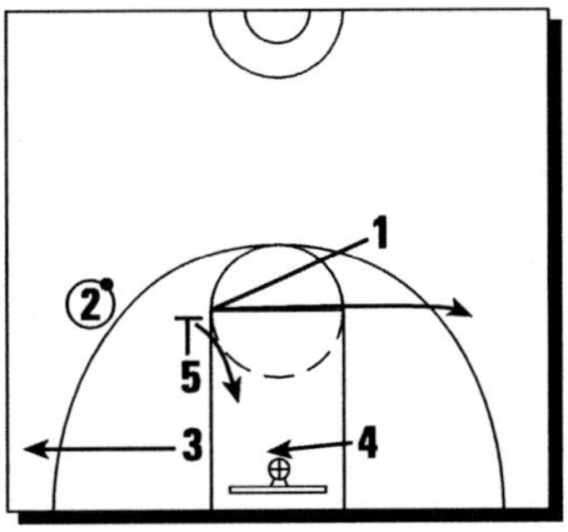

If you don't have the shot, you are back into the offense as 3 comes across.

CHAPTER 9

A FAST BREAK FOR ALL PEOPLE

Dawson Pikey

I coached for 20 years, 19 years with boys at the high school level, and one year with junior college women. The most enjoyable year was the year I coached women. I heard a couple of things at this clinic that I sincerely believe. Jane Albright-Dieterle spoke about *being yourself.* Joe Ciampi talked about the fact that you must believe in the things you do. Most of the things that we did, we did to survive. I coached in an all-white, affluent high school of 650 students, nine through twelve. Ninety to ninety-five percent of our students went on to college so I had some very bright kids, but I did not have very big kids. They didn't jump or shoot very well, nor were they very fast. With that background, you would ask how we could fast break?

I went to a clinic and heard Sonny Allen, who coached at Old Dominion. I took some of his ideas and adapted them to my small kids. I will show you my fast break and then come back and break it into parts. Then, I will show you how we used it to *counter pressure.* Once we implemented the break, the program got better every year. In our best year, we were 29 and 3 and went to the final four in the state tournament. We were the smallest team in the tournament, got beat by the team that won it, and played them a closer game than anyone.

DIAGRAM 9-1.

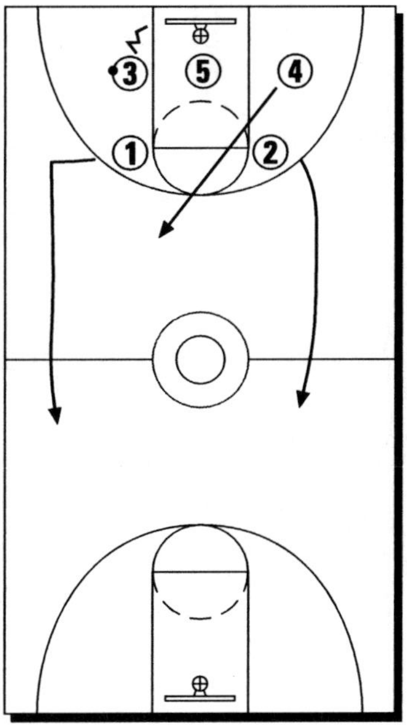

For simplicity, I am going to teach this out of a 2-3 zone, but if you ran a man-to-man or another type of zone, you could do the same thing. 1 and 2 are the guards, 5 is the center. The rebounder, 3, brings the ball down quickly, half pivots and starts a power dribble away from the basket. 3 could not take more than three dribbles. Ideally, we wanted 3 to take a line to where the half-court line met the sideline. This would differ depending on where the rebound was, but this was the optimum.

At the same time, when we saw we were going to get the rebound, we released the weakside guard, 2. We wanted 2 to go all the way to the sideline.

We are trying to outnumber the defense. You want to get down the floor first. The person who is farthest away from the board, 4 or 5, in this case 4, came to this position. 4 is in a lane outside of the free-throw lane extended. As we powered out, 3 first looked for the *deep pass.*

We taught two types of passes, either the *two-handed chest pass* or a *baseball pass* on the run. We told 3 to find the basket on the other end. 3's eyes are going to the basket on the other end; the shoulders are square. 3 can make a two-handed chest pass, which is what we did with the girls, or the baseball type pass. Remember that when you are throwing the pass, it cannot be a *flat pass.* As you make the pass, you must get *arch* over the middle of the court. The first option is the pass from 3 to 2.

The second option is the pass to 4, the *relay man.* The third option is to 1. 1 comes straight out at the free-throw line extended and then adjusts down the floor depending on where the dribbler is. 1 is the safety valve. If the dribbler comes toward 1, 1 releases accordingly. We maintain a 15-foot spacing between 3 and 1.

DIAGRAM 9-2.

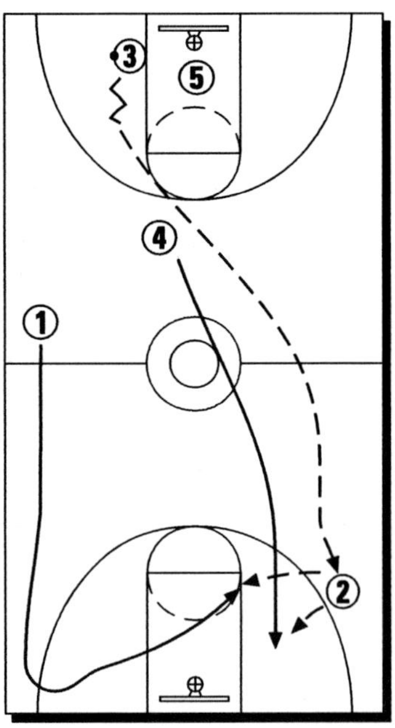

The pass is not released to the 10- second line; it is not released and "let's see what happens." It is a commitment that 2 is gone. If the pass is intercepted, 2 stays at the other end of the floor. If the opponents scored, we step out and make the *long* pass and score anyway.

We would play 4-on-4 if intercepted, because they would always keep someone back. We felt we didn't lose anything. 4 goes to the *ballside block* and looks for the pass from 2. On the pass to 2, 1 releases and runs to rebound. If 2 does not shoot, 1 breaks to the high post for a pass from 2. That's the *primary and secondary* phases of the break.

DIAGRAM 9-3.

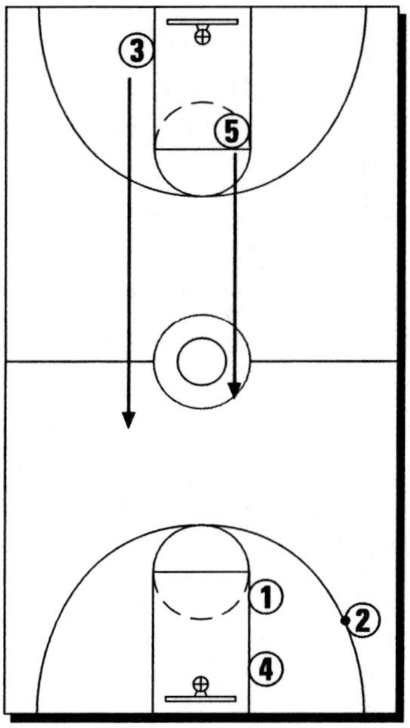

3 and 5 are coming as *trailers.* Their positions are dictated by where the defense is rather than ball location.

DIAGRAM 9-4.

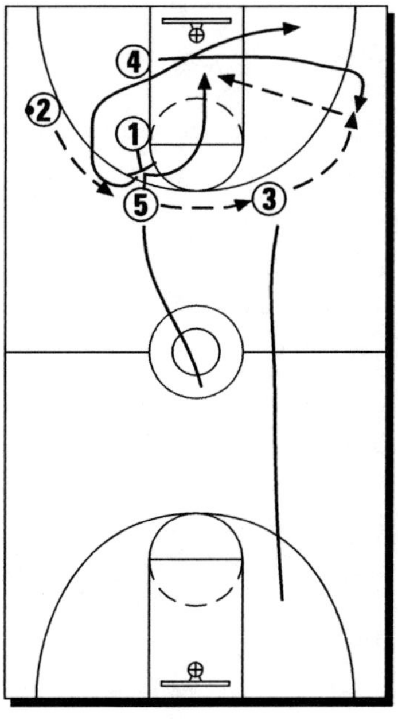

We want to get into a quick half-court offense before the defense can set up. We have a *quick turnover offense,* the third phase. If 4 does not get the pass from 2, the ball is reversed. 4 rolls to the other side of the floor. 1 sets a backpick for 5, and 5 goes to the post position on the other side of the floor. 1 would then come to the other side of the floor. The ball went 2-5-3-4-5 or 2-5-3-4-1. This is the *initial break* off of a missed shot.

DIAGRAM 9-5.

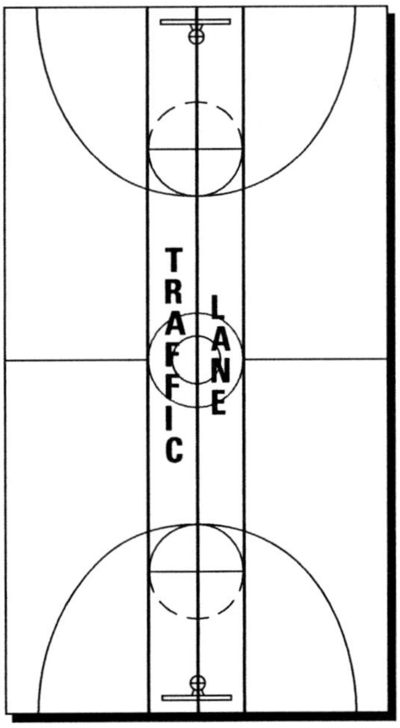

Usually the defensive players were in the traffic lane. No matter which level, that's where you find them. It never made sense to me to get the ball to the middle. There is probably nothing about rebounding I haven't tried. The most successful thing was that I quit trying to *block off.* I would block off *chest-to-chest.* We tried everything, even double-teaming on the rebound. I found out that no matter what I did, five big kids against my five little kids, they would get the ball because officials don't call the foul with the hip.

As an offensive rebounder, you can get your hip on the defense and sort of walk yourself in behind the defense. But, when we started releasing, it relieved pressure because our opponents started rebounding just three people. The first game we used this, no one knew. We had not done this the year before. We were in a tournament, not seeded, and we were up 30 points by half.

DIAGRAM 9-6.

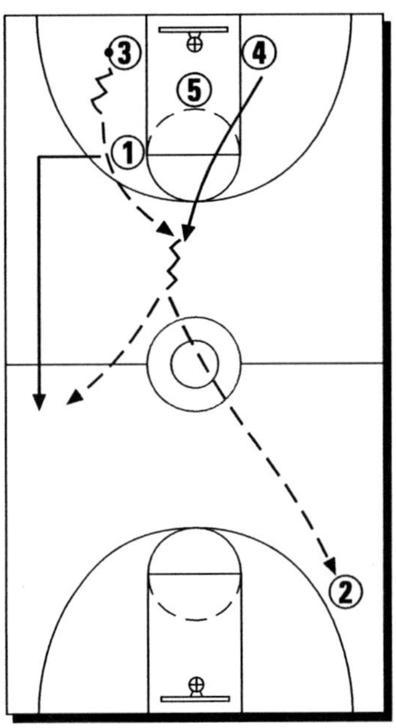

If 3 cannot pass to 2, the second option is 4. 4 also has a maximum dribble of three, but it might only be one. 4 then passes ahead to 2, or as 1 sees what is happening and breaks down the sideline, 4 can pass to 1.

DIAGRAM 9-7.

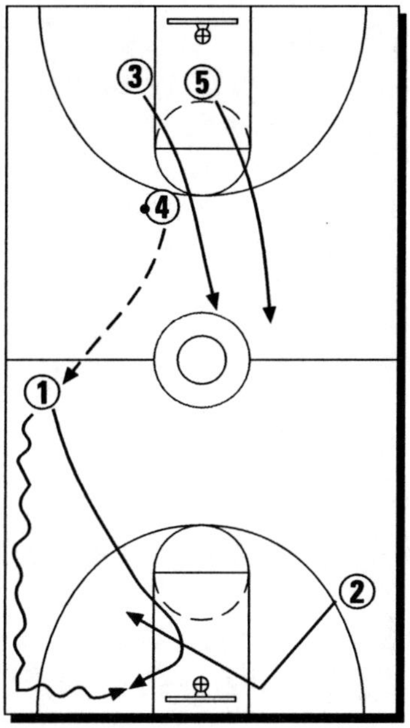

Suppose 4 passes to 1. We then do the opposite. 1 and 2 are both offensive threats. 1 will not pull up and stop. 1 will keep the ball and go as far as he can. At some point, 1 must decide whether he is going to shoot it or pass it. 1 doesn't come down and stop in a non-threatening area. 1 has the ball; 2 will break to the high post and 4 will go to the *block on the ballside.*

DIAGRAM 9-8.

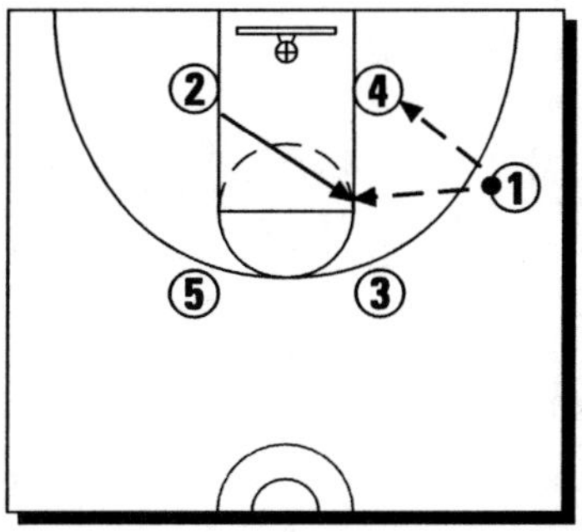

3 and 5 will be trailers, and we are set up for the turnover.

DIAGRAM 9-9.

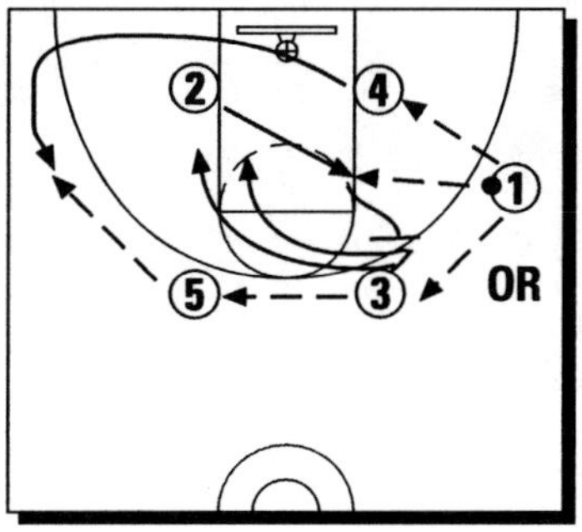

Let's turn it over. The ball will go 1-3-5-4. Meanwhile, 2 will backscreen for 3, who will go to the *ballside block.* 2 then rolls across the lane to the high-post area. If 4 doesn't have a shot, 4 can pass to either 3 or 2. Stress to your players that the pass from 3 to 5 is not a lateral pass. It is passed back at an angle so that it can't be intercepted. That's the big picture.

DIAGRAM 9-10.

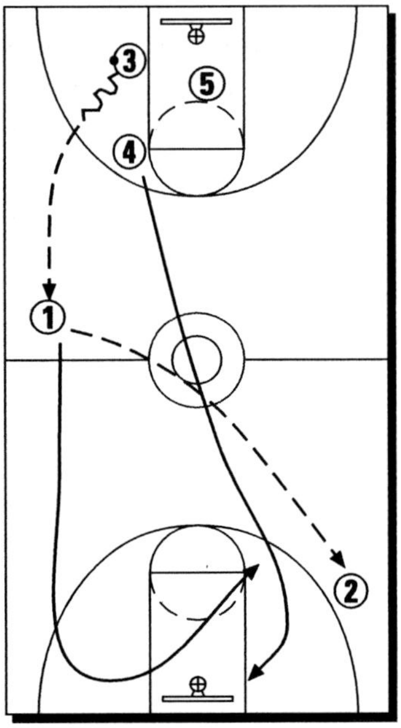

If 3 dribbles out and passes to 1,we have the same thing. We have the same options. If 1 passes to 2, 4 goes ballside block, and 1 breaks to the high-post area ball side. This is on a missed shot when we got the rebound, and we will do the same thing if it is a made shot. We will also do the same thing off both a missed free throw and a made free throw.

I'd like to show you some of the drills that we used. The very first day of our practice, we hoped that they had done something prior to the season. We started working on passing — bounce passing, chest passing, and baseball passing. We would make the sharp 15-foot passes, and then we would widen out first to 20-foot passes and then to 30-foot passes.

DIAGRAM 9-11.

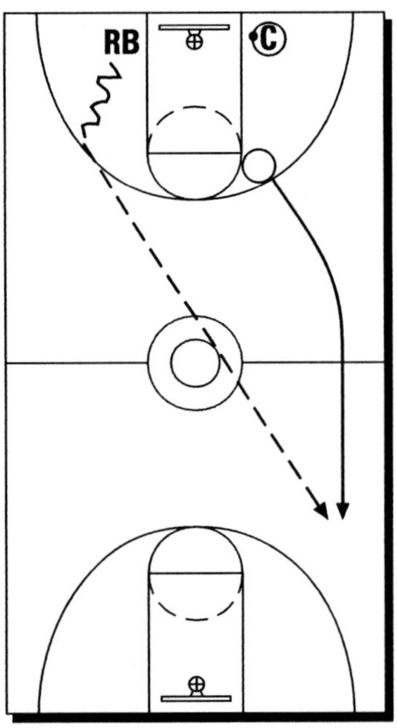

A coach throws the ball off of the board. The rebounder would *power out* on the dribble, and the other man would *release* for the pass from the rebounder. Teaching points are the *pass* and the *power dribble* being under control. Remember the *arch*, they cannot throw a *bullet pass.* Sometimes, I would have a manager stand in the middle of the floor to make sure the pass was thrown high enough.

DIAGRAM 9-12.

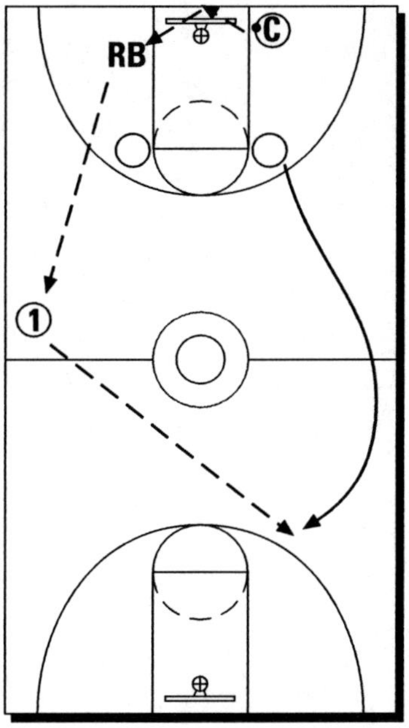

At this point, another player is added. The rebounder makes the *shorter* pass, and that player would make the long pass. We want the person who is throwing the longer pass to make the pass from the dribble.

DIAGRAM 9-13.

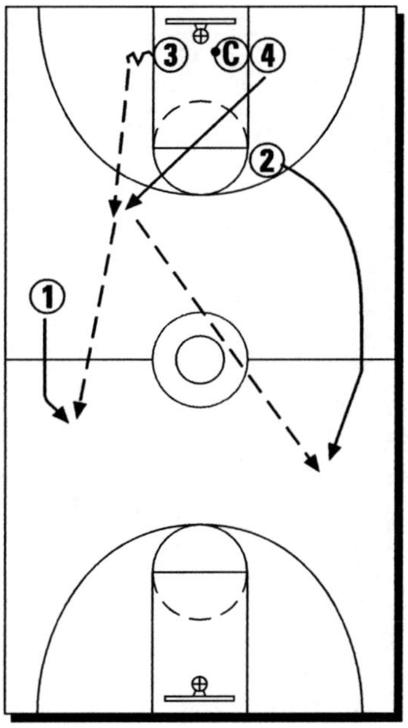

Next, we would work the drill with three options; 3 rebounds and then passes to 4 who then passes to either 1 or to 2. We would call out which option we wanted, the pass to either 1, 2, or 4.

DIAGRAM 9-14.

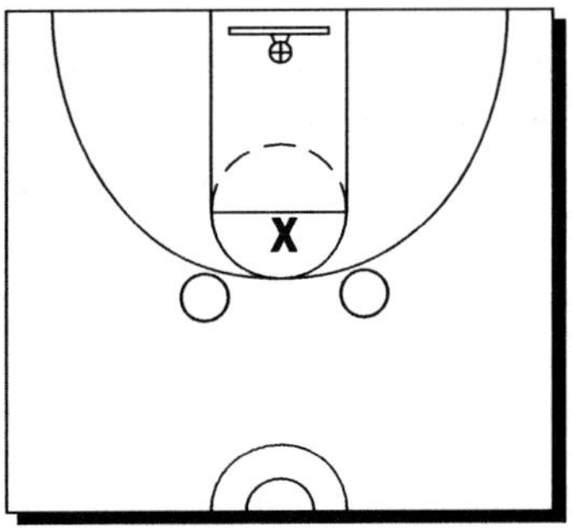

Then, another person is added on defense. You probably had your two players on a 2-on-1 situation passing the ball back and forth as they were near the middle of the court. The defensive player was usually between the man with the ball and the man who was receiving the ball. The offensive player had to pass the ball by the defensive player. I asked myself, "Why do I want to create an obstacle for the passer?"

DIAGRAM 9-15.

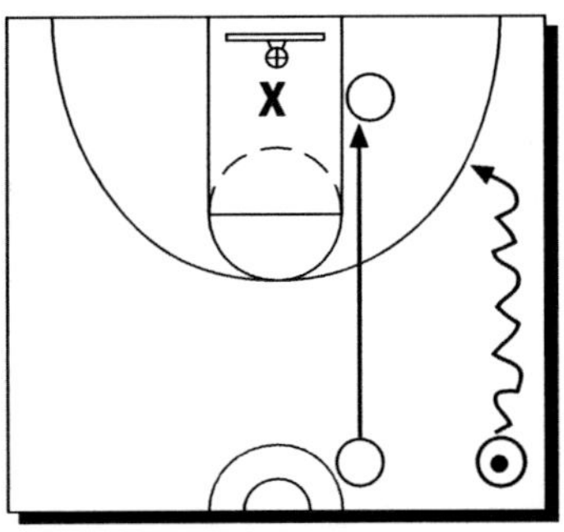

That got me to the sideline. I wanted the ball on the sideline and my second man on the 2-on-1 situation on the same side of the floor that the ball was on. We are no longer passing the ball through an obstacle. The defensive man must make a decision. Most coaches tell the defensive player to protect the basket first. The defensive player will probably defend the player on the *block.* That gives the player with the ball an open shot.

DIAGRAM 9-16.

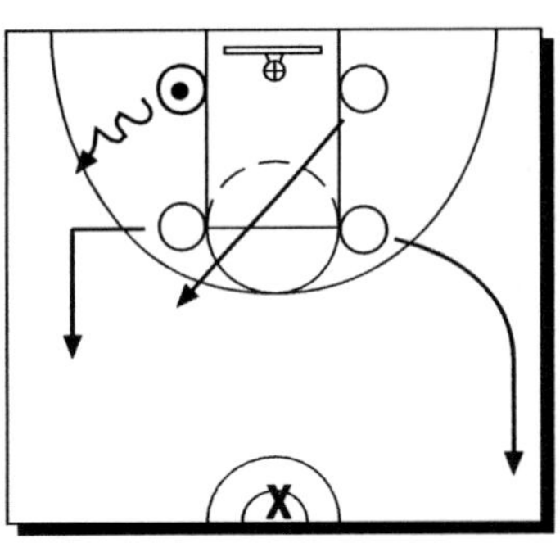

We run this drill with one defensive player starting at mid-court. We go 4-on-1. I wanted to make sure that we scored. How do you teach your defensive player to react when it is 3-on-1?

DIAGRAM 9-17.

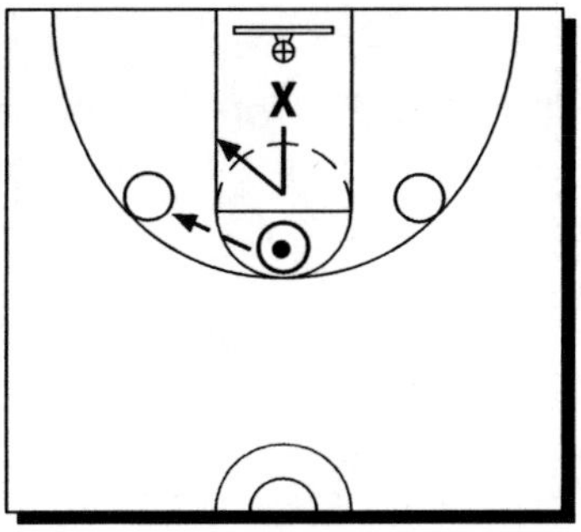

Here's the type of 3-on-1 you are usually facing. I taught the defensive man to *challenge* the ball and get the man with the ball to *stop dribbling,* and then react to the pass, and hope that by then you had help.

DIAGRAM 9-18.

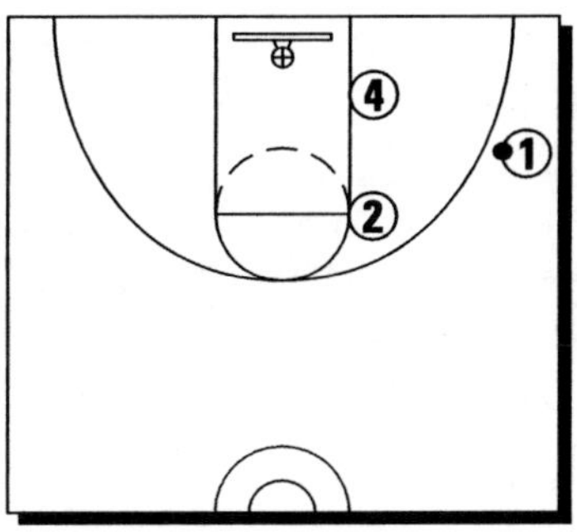

By getting 3-on-1 on the side with the ball in the corner, a player at the block and another at the high post, you probably won't make a pass.

DIAGRAM 9-19.

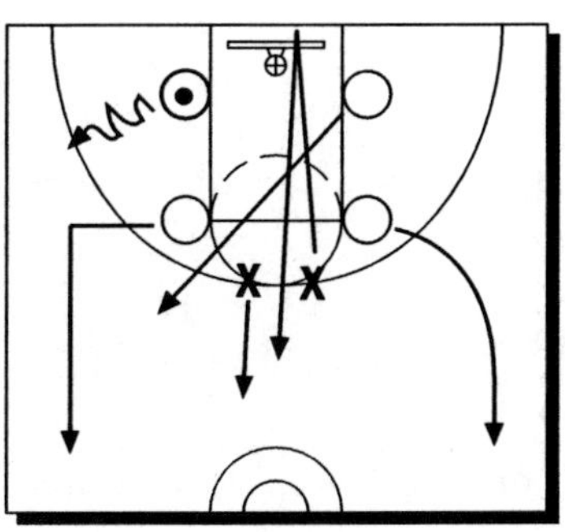

Let's add a *second defensive player.* Both start at the head of the key, and on the rebound, one defensive player had to touch the end line and then get into the action.

DIAGRAM 9-20.

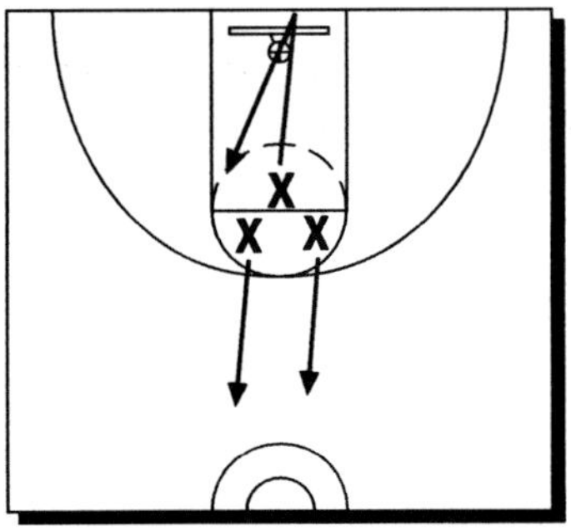

A *third defensive player* is then added. We are showing this for clarification only to the right.

DIAGRAM 9-21.

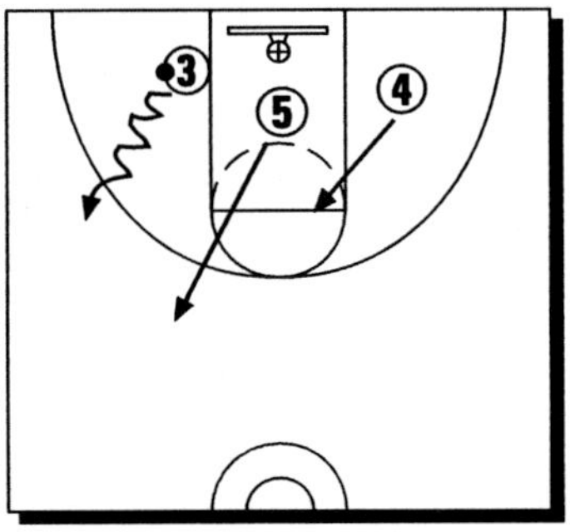

If 3 rebounds, 5 possibly can get to the position shown for 4. If either 4 or 5 can see the other person in front of him, it is the other person's lane. 5 moves to ballside to rebound and would not get to that lane first.

DIAGRAM 9-22.

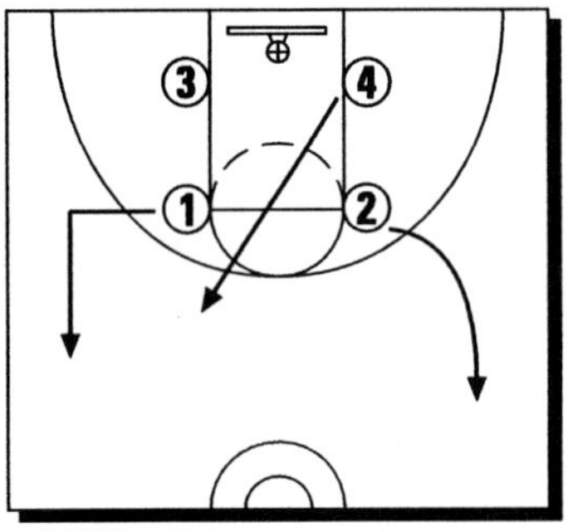

If 5 rebounds, he *powers out,* taking 3's spot. But since 5 is in the middle of traffic, usually his method of releasing the ball was a pass to 1. Many times, if 5 got the rebound, we didn't have the break. Sometimes, 5 might hit 4 at the top of the circle.

DIAGRAM 9-23.

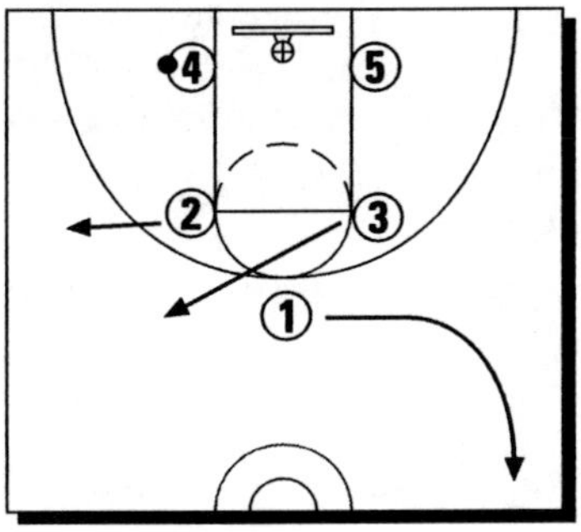

You can run this from a 1-2-2 zone. Diagram 9-23 shows 4 rebounding. 1 is almost the designated *release man.*

DIAGRAM 9-24.

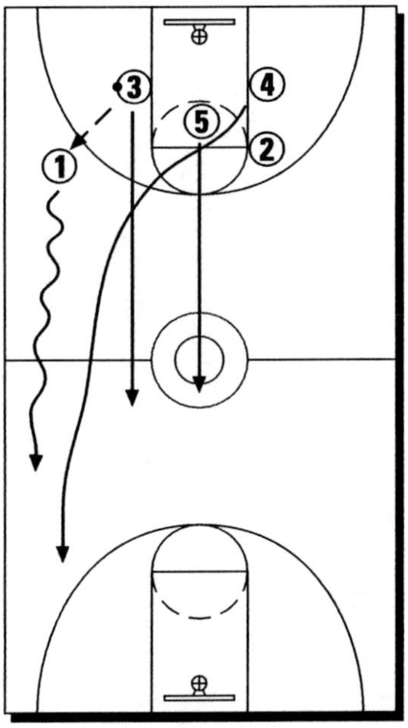

Suppose the pass is made to 1, and he cannot make the next pass. 4 goes to the *low block,* 2 *releases* and then *breaks* to the high post. 1 dribbles as far down the floor as he can. 3 and 5 will be the trailers.

DIAGRAM 9-25.

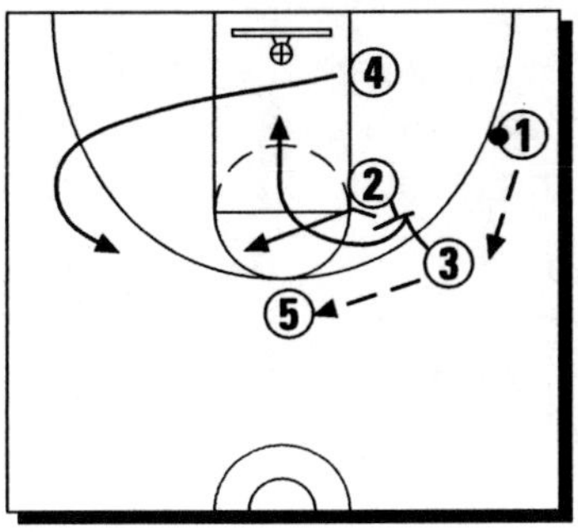

If 1 cannot get the shot, the ball is reversed to 3 to 5. 2 back-screens for 3 who breaks low. 4 crosses the lane and breaks wide, and 2 then rolls high. The ball goes 1-3-5-4-3 or 1-3-5-4-2.

DIAGRAM 9-26.

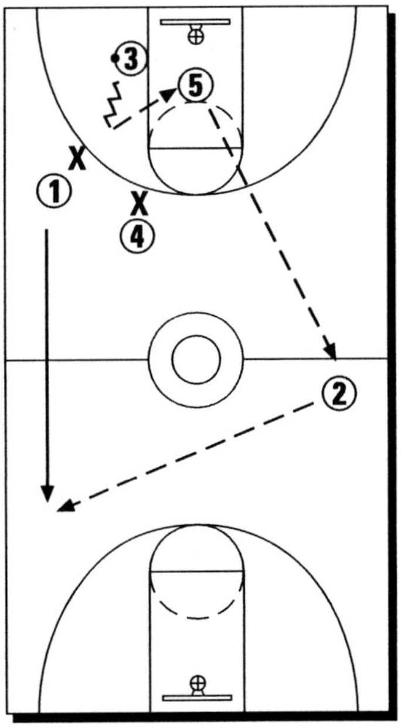

If 1 and 4 are both defended and 3 cannot pass to 2 from the power dribble, 3 doesn't dribble because he isn't a good ballhandler. 3 passes back to 5; 2 comes back to relieve the pressure. 1 can release with 2 passing to 1.

DIAGRAM 9-27.

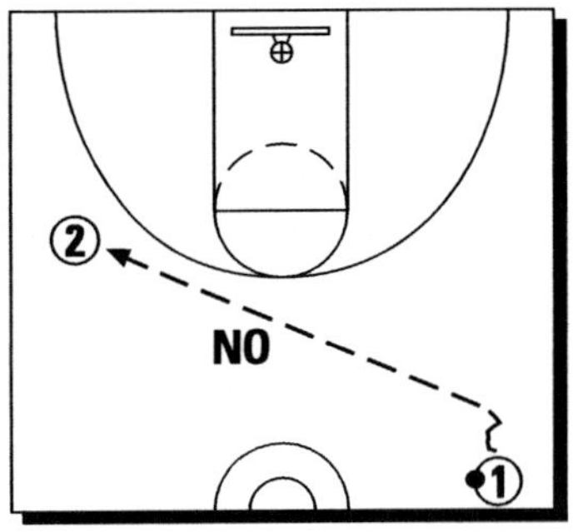

The following teaching point is important. Once the ball comes across the 10-second line, percentage wise, forget the cross-court pass because the defense is back, and it is difficult to get the arched pass crosscourt.

DIAGRAM 9-28.

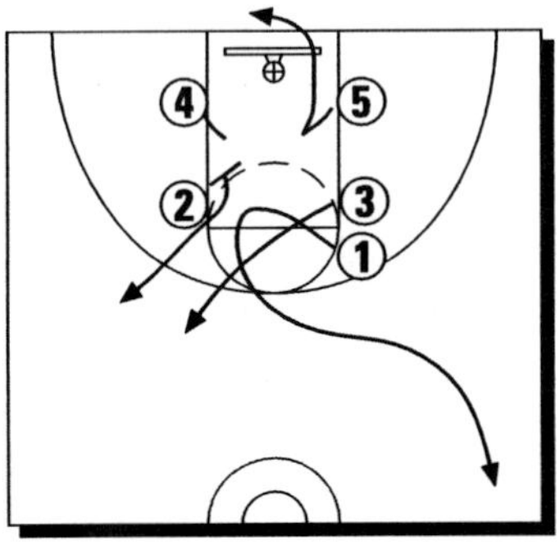

The break from the made or missed free throw. We want our best passer at 5. We rebound five people because we are small, and we want to make certain we do not give up an offensive rebound. We work at *blocking off.* 1 blocks the shooter and then *releases.* Off the made shot, 5 takes the ball out of the net, and doesn't let it hit the floor. As 5 goes out-ofbounds, he turns and looks down the floor. The ball is back and ready to be thrown. 2 is the outlet; 3 is the middleman. Nothing has changed. If we are down several points with a few seconds to play, we don't call a special play; we run this, something that we have been running all year. This is our *last-second play.*

DIAGRAM 9-29. BREAK THE PRESS

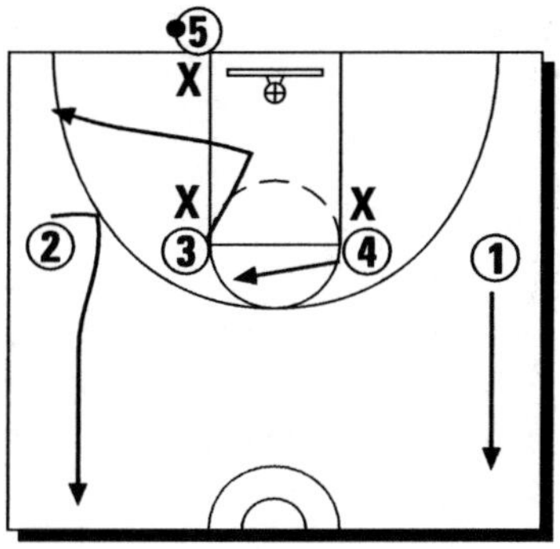

We line up in a 1-4 vs 1-2-1-1 press. We run our fast break. 1 and 2 are guards. We spread the floor with 3 and 4 at the elbows. 3 breaks up and toward the corner. We fake to 3. 1 is the release man. 4 comes into the hole vacated by 3. 2 jockeys for position in the release area.

DIAGRAM 9-30.

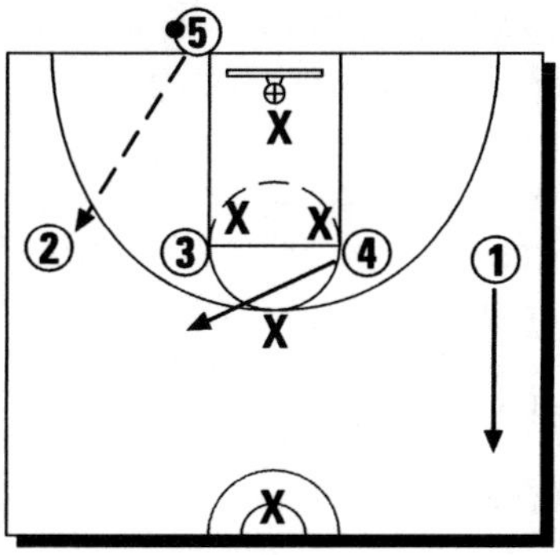

If 5 passes to 2, 1 releases, and 4 becomes the middle man. Remember, we will have someone open. A 1-2-1-1 press must adjust to what we are doing.

DIAGRAM 9-31. 2-2-1 PRESS

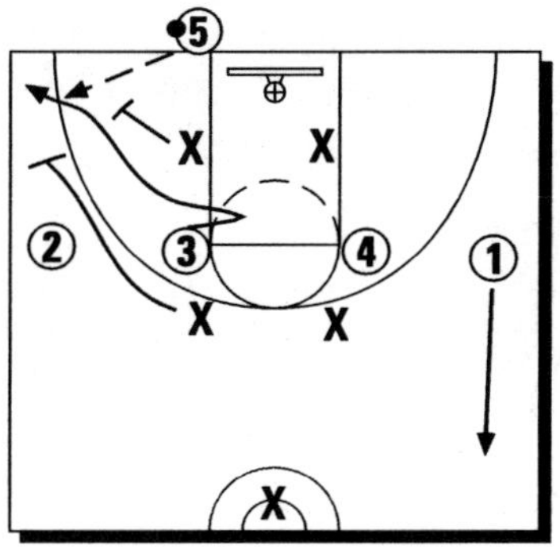

If 5 passes into the corner because 3 was left open, 3 would make an *arching pass* to 2 as the trap materialized. We really didn't like the pass made into the corner, but sometimes it happened.

CHAPTER 10

TIGER FAST BREAK

Jo Ann Rutherford

Until you establish a philosophy, you really can't do much. When we come to clinics, we want to see some X's and O's, but we all know most of that. What is crucial is how we implement it into our system. Many coaches will look at their players and say, "How can we run?" You may have short, slow players. Whatever type of players you have, if you want to implement the fast break into your system, you can. It's just a matter of where you want to put them. We have players at Missouri who are not very tall. Our tallest player is 6'2". We don't have great athletes; hard workers, yes, but not great athletes.

The first thing we do is start with our weight program. If your players can jump, run, move, are strong, and have a good range of motion, you are going to have a better athlete. If you can get your players involved in a weight program, even one or two days a week, it is going to help them. Also, we do everything quick. We time everything. In a fast break, you must make decisions, and you must make them quickly. So, from day one, I want them making decisions under pressure. And that's exactly what a fast break is.

We start with *conditioning.* We started out by having the guards run the distances in a certain time, the forwards had their time and the posts theirs. One of my post players came to me and said, "Coach, we're only 6' 1", why can we run with the others?" And it came to me that when you start labeling your players, you are saying to them that some are slower. Now, we avoid doing that. We want our guards to be the best; they must be out front. We do speed work in our conditioning. We do a six-minute mile, but after that, 220 is our longest distance. We do short distance work, time world, and sprints. You must get them in the proper mentality. If you are going to put in a fast-break offense and your defense is a set zone, I think the transition is so hard from the fast break to a stand-up zone or a set offense. We run directly from the fast break into a *secondary offense or a motion or a flex offense.* You have your movement going before the defense sets. Defensively, we like to play *man press,* up-tempo.

Everything in our program is part of one extended philosophy. That doesn't mean that we don't play some match-ups; we don't ever play some zone. But, it's difficult to have one philosophy on one end of the floor and another philosophy on the other end. Do your players like to run? We try to do as much running as we can, making it fun. We do as much as we can on the court with the ball. I don't just sprint. I want them making decisions. We do other types of running. We do cross training, parachute work, anything that you can use that doesn't seem like running to them. We play *frisbee* in post season. We do a lot of *juggling* for hand-eye coordination. If you have a player who has poor hand-eye coordination, get them three *tennis balls.* They love it. How many of your athletes have *proper technique* in running? The first thing we do is to spend some time with the track coach to go over the basic mechanics of running properly.

We go over eight basic skills with our players:

- *Running* — What is the proper running position — stride, arms, breathing, leaning, the whole synopsis of what we want them to do?
- *Jumping* — arms, leg position, stride, the proper technique. Some players don't know how to jump. We do plyometrics; we do a lot with boxes. Get your shop to make them.
- *Pivoting* — especially in a fast break offense.
- *Passing* — spend a lot of time with that. They must make decisions when they pass.
- *Rebounding* — Have them take a ball, hold their arms straight up and have them pass it back and forth going up and down the floor. How long can they do that? They will not be able to do it for a minute. How much work can they do with outlet passing and rebounding if they can't hold up their arms for a minute? So, we try to spend some time developing upper body strength.
- *Catching* — hands up. We never drop the hands. We do not drop the hands after we make a pass. The hands stay up, with the thumbs up. The hands are always in the ready position.
- *Dribbling* — Who can handle the ball? We want the guards to be the best ballhandlers. But, we let our forwards and post handle the ball if it is the last resort. When we fill lanes, we don't assign lanes. When we started this, we assigned lanes, but the players seemed to have an excuse why they couldn't get there so we just started filling lanes by positions.
- *Shooting* — get the shot that you want to use out of the break (e.g., right- and left-handed layups, power layups, free-throw line, backboard shot). Those are your main shots off the break. Those are the four main shots we want off the break. These eight basic skills are everything we implement from day one. If you have a player who can do these eight things, you have a player.

During practice we chart everything, makes and misses. At the end of practice, we know how many layups you made and how many you missed. I think an athlete needs to know what they are doing well and what they are doing poorly. I ask a player in the gym how many shots she took and how many she made, and she doesn't know. How does she know that she is getting any better? We have more of a controlled break with all five people running. We want everyone filling lanes. We don't want anyone lying back. We put the 4 and 5 players in the drills.

DIAGRAM 10-1.

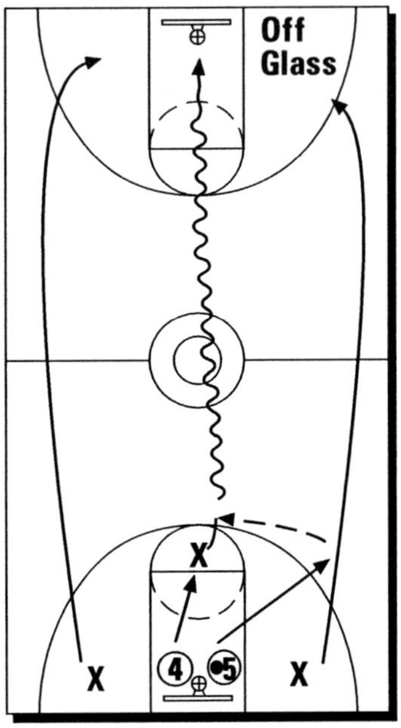

Our first pass goes to the *outlet side*, and then into the middle. It may go back to the outlet and back to the middle again. When the middle person gets to the free-throw line, she throws the ball off the glass. 4 must come in and tip it back on the glass, and 5 then puts it in. So, 4 and 5 are trailers, and make sure they are in the fast-break drills. We have five players running, and we want to get the ball up the floor as quickly as possible.

DIAGRAM 10-2.

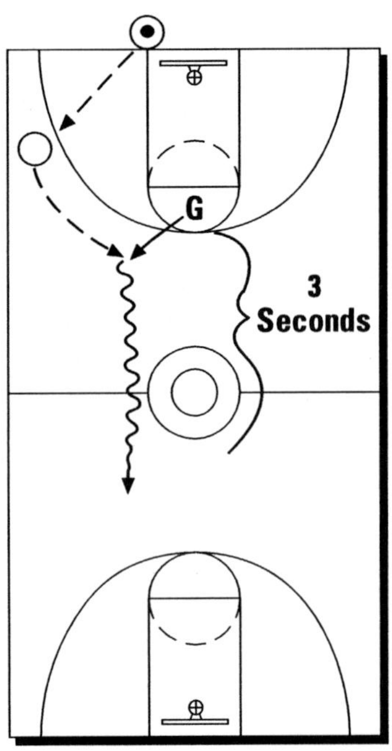

If the outlet pass is made at this point, we want to get the ball into the middle as quickly as possible. When this happens, it is the key for the other people to fill the lanes. We say that nothing happens between the tops of the circles. You should be able to cover this distance in three seconds. You don't want to waste this time.

DIAGRAM 10-3.

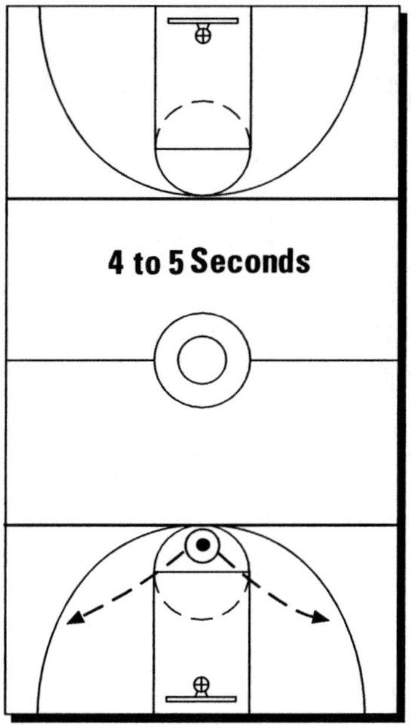

The next distance is to the top of the free-throw line where the guard stops. The ball should be passed to the wing position in four or five seconds at most. We never make a *blind pass,* and once within the scoring area, the player in the middle becomes the key. You must have a guard who makes good decisions.

DIAGRAM 10-4.

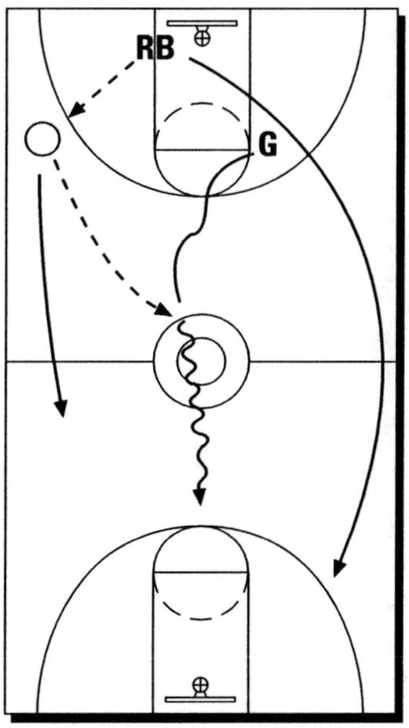

How do we decide who fills? The shot is missed and rebounded. The rebounder always fills the opposite lane. The outlet makes the pass to the center and fills the other outside lane. The guard is in the middle. 4 and 5 fill in between. What if the guard gets the rebound? Same thing. The guard outlets, and the other person fills the middle. Most of the time your guard will have the ball. You must have *talking guards.* The guard must be the leader, directing the players. I like a *verbal* team. Something else. If you start getting a lot of turnovers, don't panic. Don't give up the break. Keep working with it.

Question — We have a lot of trouble with the second pass, with the turnover with the guard moving away. What do you do about that?

Answer—DIAGRAM 10-5.

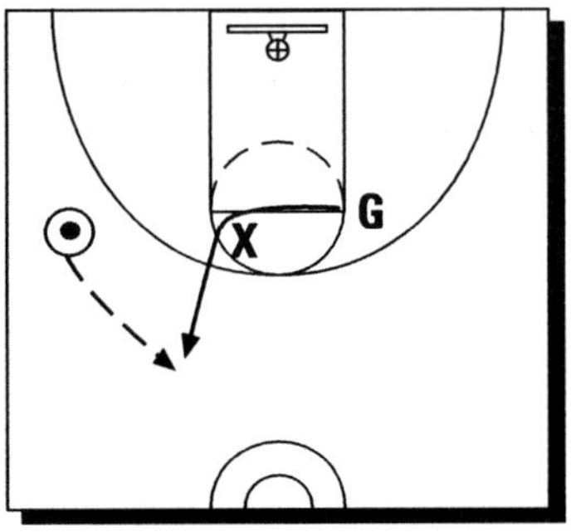

You must always teach your guard to *cut* to the ball and make sure that there is no defensive player between the outlet and the guard. The guard must cut in front of the defense and go to the ball. That is her responsibility. And if the defense is cheating, she must *fake and go long.* She must read this. Sometimes she must come all the way to the sideline to get the pass. If she does, then someone else will fill middle.

The outlet must have her hand up, make a V-cut, and call for the ball. She must be moving to help the rebounder. You should make sure that your rebounder turns the right way. If she is on the right side of the basket, she turns right; if she is on the left side of the basket, she turns left. She doesn't pass across the court. If the ball comes off in the middle, she can go to either side. We do everything full-court. We do some 3-on-2, 2-on-1, and 4-on-2 situations where they must know where the defense is. This is decision- making.

DIAGRAM 10-6.

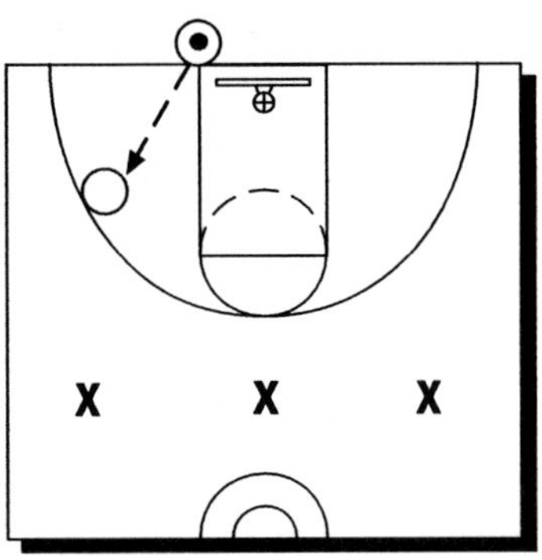

I'll use three people, not 4 and 5. I'll set three defensive players near mid-court. The ball is thrown off the glass, rebounded and the outlet pass made. Then, the three offensive players will go full- court against these three.

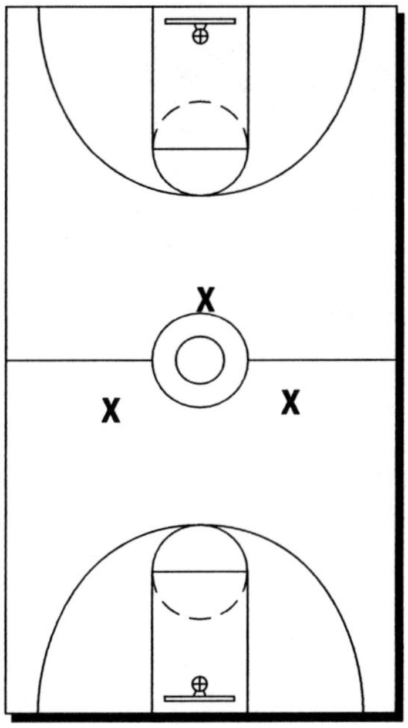

The next time, one defender is up, two are back (Diagram 10-7).

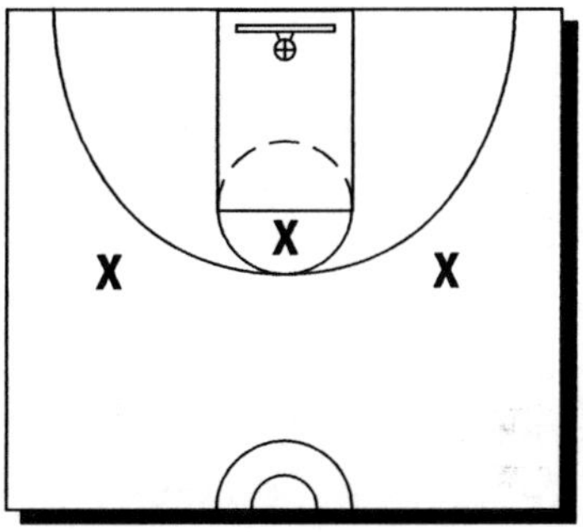

Next, three players will be up. We will vary the situations so the offensive team running must react to them. Even if we see a half-court defense, we will not give up the break (Diagram 10-8).

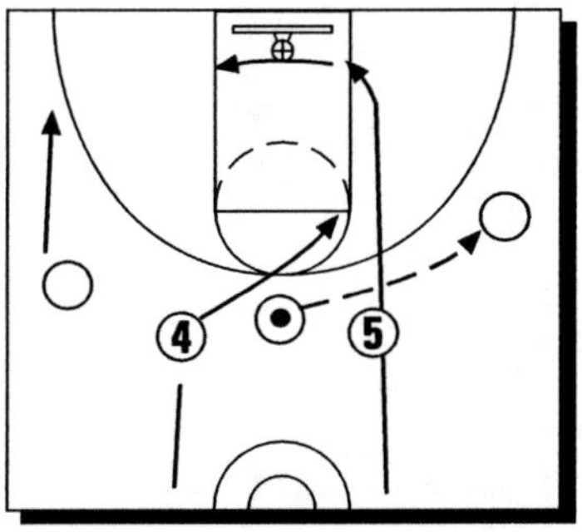

Suppose we don't have the break. 4 and 5 are trailers. We are 5-on-3, but no break. The ball is passed to the wing. 5 goes to the block on the ballside. If she doesn't get the ball, she clears. 4 follows (Diagram 10-9).

If 4 doesn't get the ball, she screens away for 5. We want to get as close to the basket as we can and get the high- percentage shot (Diagram 10-10).

CHAPTER 11

DEVELOPING THE FAST BREAK AND QUICK HIT PLAYS

PAUL WESTHEAD

This system has both a great risk for an advantage and a great risk for a disadvantage. If you are playing someone significantly better than you and both teams take the same number of shots, you will lose. If an average number of shots is 80, then to win, you either have to play slow or fast by taking either 40 shots or 120 shots.

A fast-breaking team must be a great offensive rebounding team because there will be more offensive rebounding opportunities in this system. It is a speed game where you try to run the ball down court and shoot in three seconds every time. Why take shots with five players back ready to defend when you can shoot against three, two or even one?

Most players do not want to play fast. They say they do, but they really do not. Once they slow it down, this system is done. A major problem is your own players, because they do not want to get this tired for a whole game. If they do this for a whole game, however, they will win. If they do not do it the whole game, you will lose. The enemy is your team.

FAST BREAK

When the ball goes through the net, every player knows exactly what their role is.

DIAGRAM 11-1.

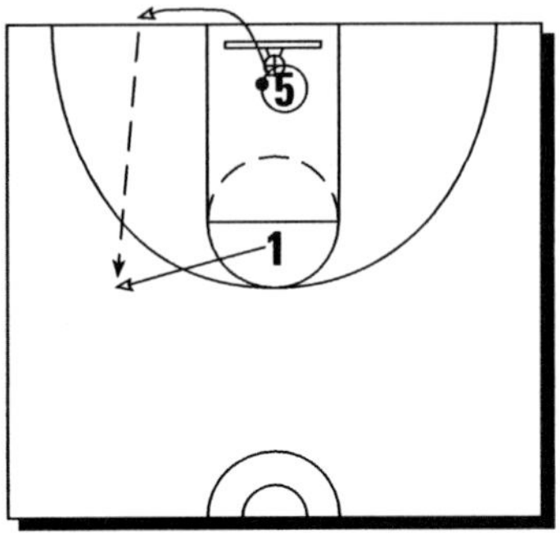

#5 man—Takes the ball out of the net. The outlet must be executed with perfection. This position cannot block out because this player has to get the ball out of the net. 1 and 5 have to execute their role automatically. They should go so fast that you do not recognize the defense.

DIAGRAM 11-2.

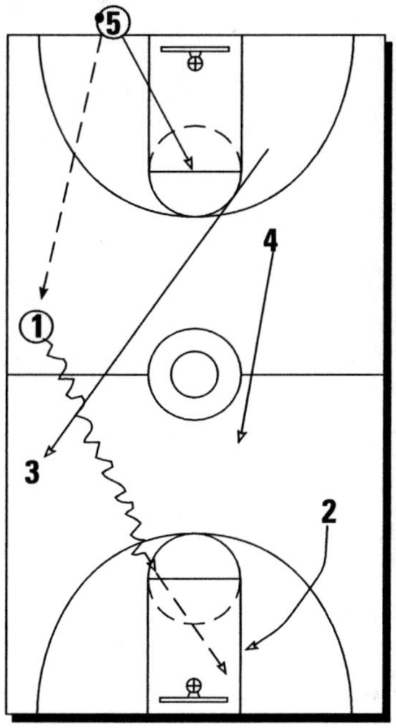

#1 man—Catches the outlet and speed dribbles to the elbow faster than anything. The faster the ball goes in the hands of 1, the faster everyone else will go. Then, you should pass for a score.

DIAGRAM 11-3.

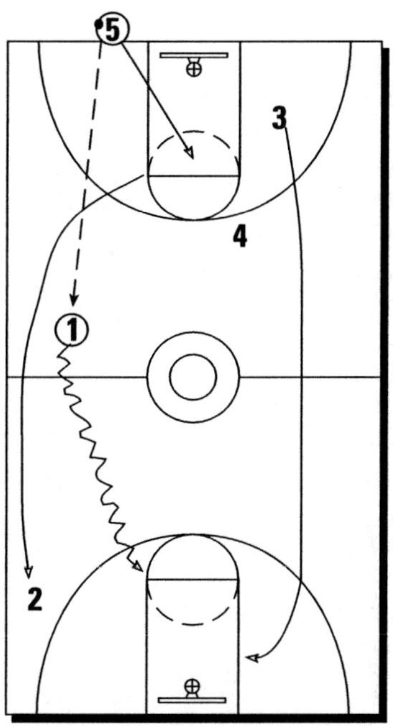

#3 man—Has to be the flat-out hardest working player. This player does not have to be a scorer, but just has to play hard all the time. There are two reasons for this: the first is to get open for a score and the other is to drag the defense for others to get open.

5-1-3 Drill—1 catches the outlet and looks for 3. Fast players may not run hard 75 times like they need to. Finding players who will play fast is a problem. Officials will sabotage the system because they do not want to run this fast. Your opposition will try to sabotage this system. But, the opponent will not run back 75 times so only you will stop you, not the opposition.

DIAGRAM 11-4.

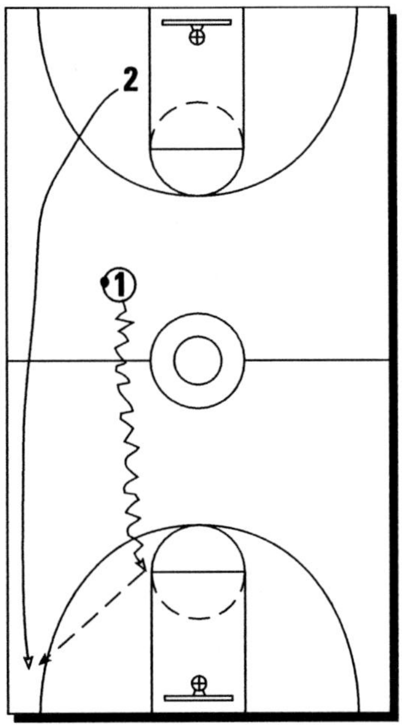

#2 man—This role is the designated shooter. This position will get 20 open shots a game. The player must sprint, spot up, catch it, and shoot it. If the player catches it and turns it over, then that player is on the bench. Shooting the ball in three seconds makes for a very low turnover ratio. Encourage them to not worry about making mistakes. Then, they will make more shots.

DIAGRAM 11-5.

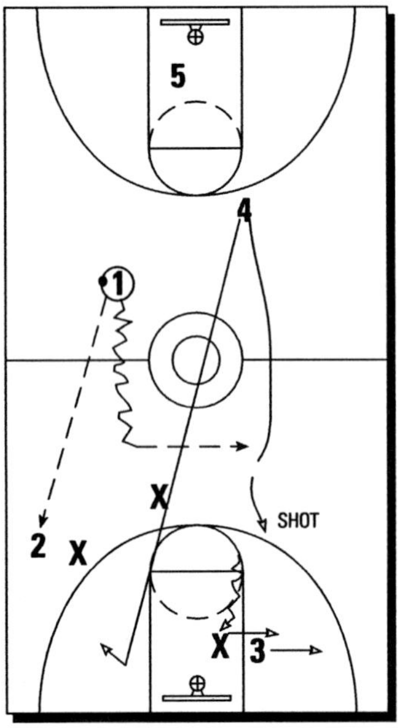

#4 man—This is your best offensive player. This position catches a pass from 1 and can shoot or drive with live ball. Any time the ball is passed ahead 1 to 2, then 4 cuts to the block. This is where the best player is getting a second look. When 4 vacates the top of the key, 5 takes that spot. 4 can use 2's shot as an opportunity to get the ball again. 2 does not have to pass to 4, but can.

DIAGRAM 11-6.

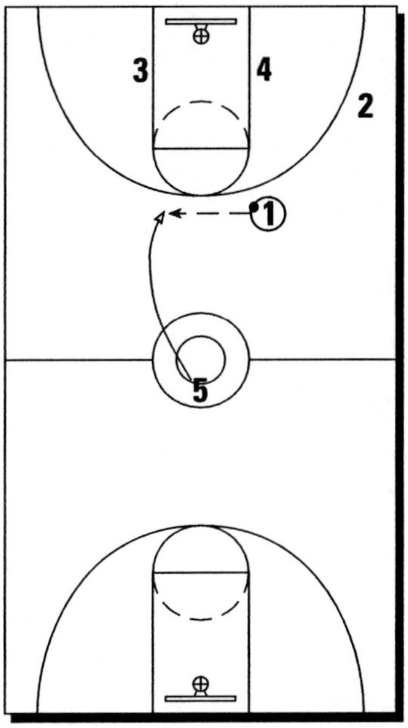

5 shoots the ball on the reverse.

DIAGRAM 11-7.

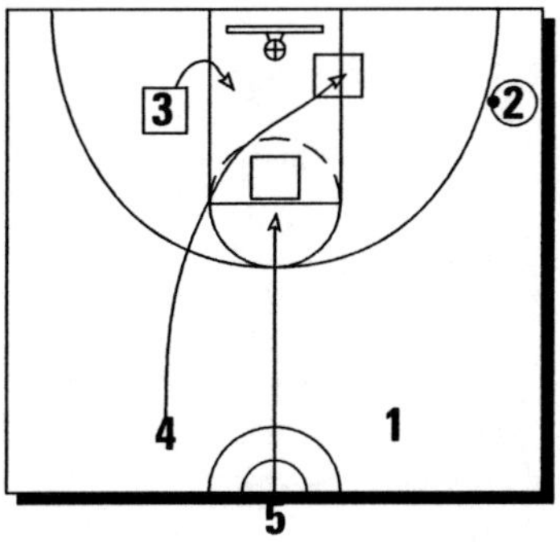

5 can also go to rebound, which gives the offense a triangle rebounding position.

DIAGRAM 11-8. 2-H

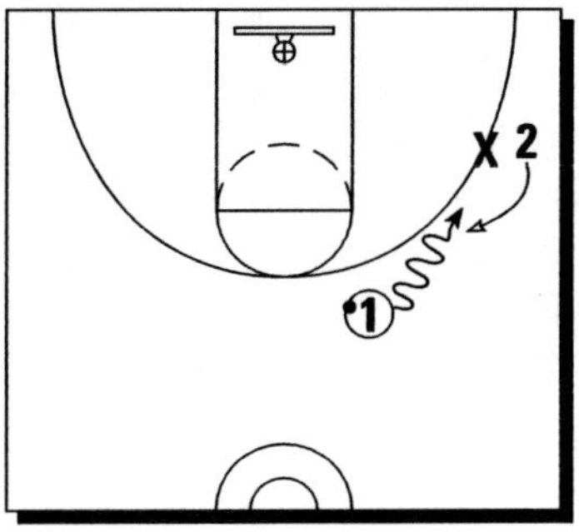

This is a handoff from 1 to 2 for a shot.

DIAGRAM 11-9. PICK AND ROLL

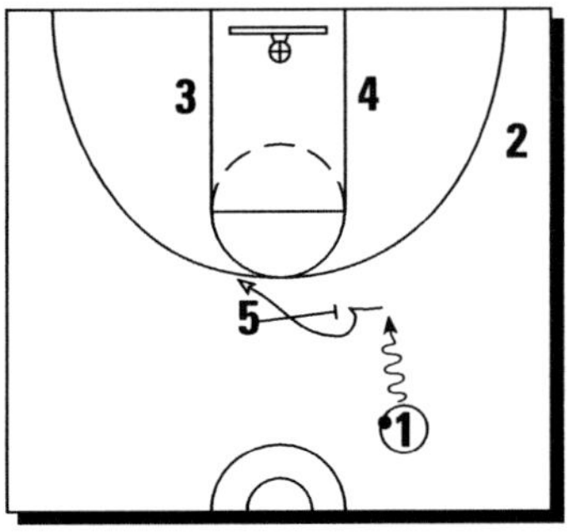

1 comes off of 5's pick to score.

DIAGRAM 11-10. 4 PICK

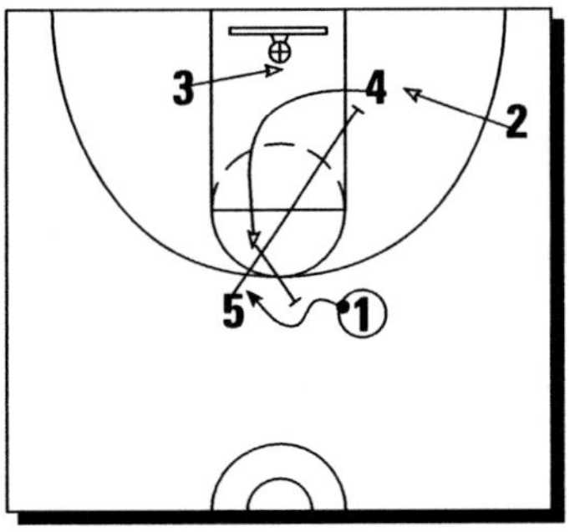

5 downscreens for 4, who then sets a ballscreen for 1 for the shot.

DIAGRAM 11-11. 3 BACK

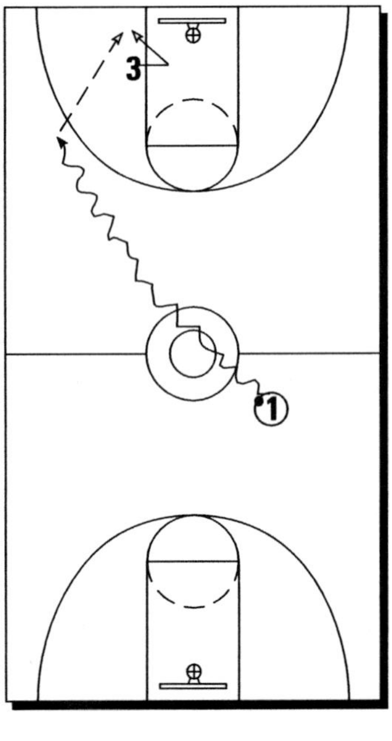

1 crosses half-court with the dribble. 3 cuts into lane, and then darts back to the block for the ball.

CHAPTER 12

THE FAST BREAK

ROY WILLIAMS

This is how we build our fast break. First of all, if you are going to do this, you must still be yourself. Secondly, don't get stuck with a system if it doesn't fit your players. Be aware that your personnel changes every year. This year we were fantastic in our *primary break.* In our *secondary break,* this was probably the worst team that we have had in four years. We had four new kids on the floor this year. You must decide whether you like this type of game or not. I love going up and down the court. The fans like it, the players like to play that way, and the only group left is the coaches, and I don't think that the game is just for our enjoyment.

When I came to Kansas, I asked what the school scoring record was, and they said "81." I said that we were going to break it, and we did. We broke it again the second year, averaging 90 points a game. And in the last two years we have been averaging 84 and 86 ppg. Since the players like to play that way, it helps us in our recruiting. Fans like it; it's entertaining.

One more thing, as a coach you have negative thoughts all the time sitting on the bench. I really do. The faster you go, the less time you have to think those negative thoughts. If you are running the break, you are four negative thoughts behind. So, we are going to play fast. I want you to understand that this is exactly what we do.

DIAGRAM 12-1. FAST BREAK DRILL #1

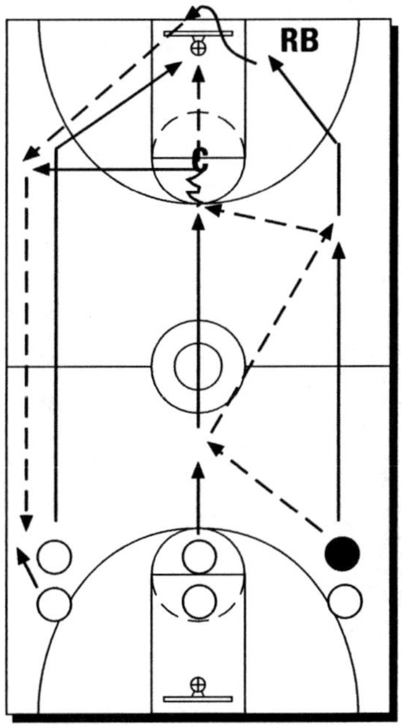

We start with three lines at the foul line extended. The first day, we have one ball, after that we have two. The ball starts on the side, with a pass to the middle man. The middle man makes the pass back, and can pass to either side. When it comes back to the middle man again, he keeps it. He must get under control to the *top of the key.* If he needs to dribble to get there, that's fine. He must stop at the foul line. We have a coach there to be sure that he stops there. He must understand that in a game, the defensive players are going to try to take the charge there. At the extended foul line, the outside players will plant their outside foot and make a 45-degree angle cut to the basket. He will pass to either side. He shoots a layup.

The other outside man is the rebounder. The middle man follows his pass. If he passes to the left, he moves to the left to the outlet spot. If the rebounder is a 4 or 5 man, he takes the ball out of bounds. If it is a 1, 2, or 3, he does not take it out of bounds. But, the rebounder makes a *two-handed overhead* outlet pass to the middle man. The middle man will then turn and make a *baseball pass* down the sideline to the next man in line. *The feed pass is a bounce pass, then we have the overhead pass, and then the baseball pass.* So, this drill is also a passing drill; bounce pass for the feed, overhead for the outlet, and then baseball pass down the side.

DIAGRAM 12-2. FAST BREAK DRILL #2

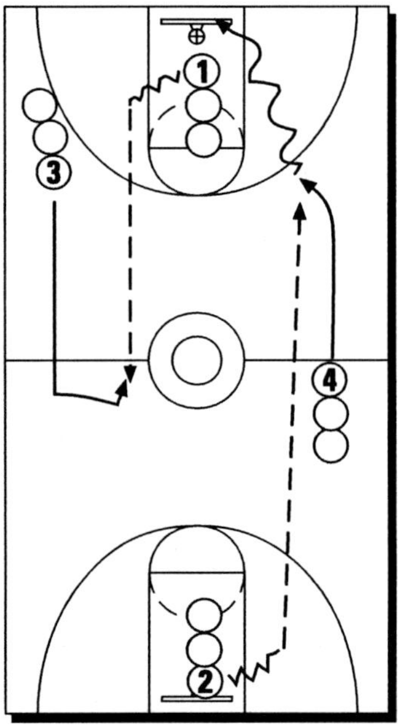

This is a *"pitch ahead"* drill. Today, we will work on the right-hand bustout. 1 puts the ball on the board and rebounds. We talk a lot about rebounding the ball in front of you. I don't like it when they rebound over their head. If you get it straight over your head, anyone has a chance to get it. We work on the box out, with the jack-knife position, and rebound the ball in front of you. It takes the player behind you out of the play. After the rebound, 1 turns and busts out, going toward the other end of the court. I want the first dribble out in *front* of the player, not on the side. We do this with everybody. They take no more than two dribbles and make the simple *pitch ahead* pass to 3. When 3 gets to midcourt, he is really going hard. 1 goes to the back of 4's line. 2 and 4 are doing the same thing. 3 goes to 2's line.

DIAGRAM 12-3. FAST BREAK DRILL #3—3/2 AND 2/1.

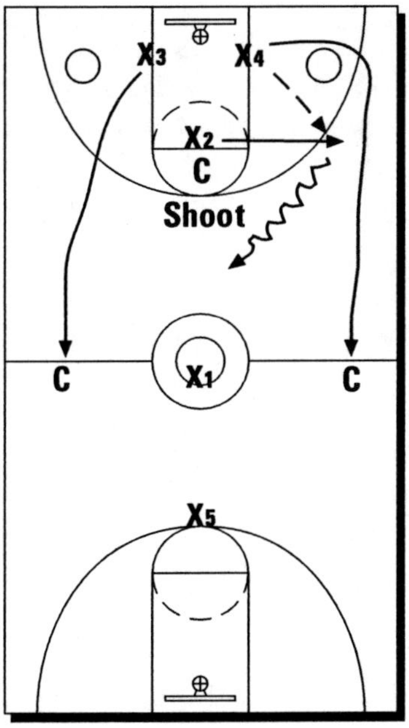

We add *boxing out* to this drill. We have three coaches on the floor for this drill. Two defenders are at halfcourt. They stay until the coach tells them to go. The coach shoots. X3 and X4 box out the offensive players; X2 boxes out the coach. If X4 rebounds, X2 must get to the outlet position. X2, X3 and X4 are now on offense. X2 goes as hard as he can into the middle on the dribble. X3 and X4 fill the lanes.

DIAGRAM 12-4.

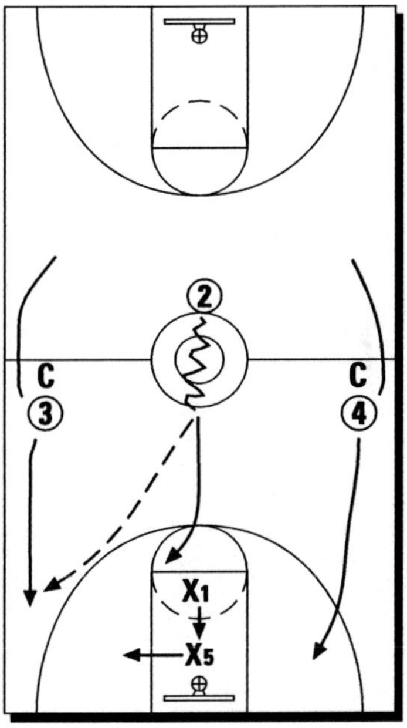

Now, 2, 3, and 4 are coming down against X1 and X5 who are in tandem. One has the hole, the other has the ball. Our rule is, if there are *two or less* defenders, we are running *primary break.* So, we must get a shot in two or less passes. We want the shot immediately. Suppose that 2 passes to 3. 2 moves to the elbow on the side of the ball. We do this because it is harder to guard. If the pass were made from 2 to 3, X5 would take the ball, and X1 would drop back opposite. So, if 3 passes back to 2, he has the shot. 3 can also pass to 4 on the *skip-pass*, and then 4 would shoot. Remember, two or less defenders, we want a shot in two or less passes.

DIAGRAM 12-5.

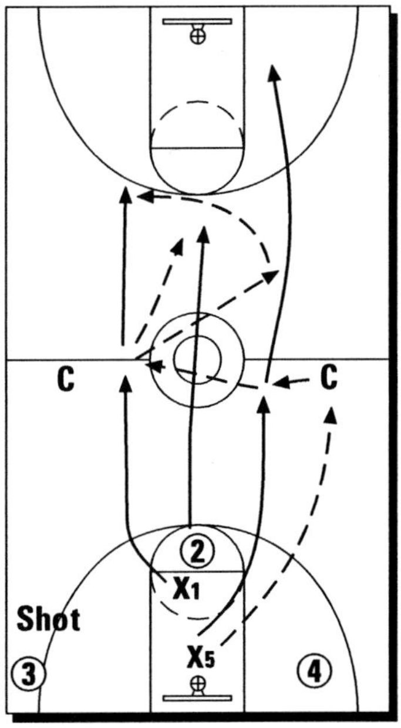

Let's say 3 shoots it. We are now going 2-on-1 the other way. Suppose X5 gets the rebound. He must outlet to the coach on his side. Now, the original middle-man is on defense. So, X1 and X5 are coming back against 2. With a 2-on-1, we want the ball passed back and forth. Make the defensive man make a decision at the foul line. If you have the ball, is he going to play you or is he going to play the other man? If he is playing the other man, take one more dribble and lay it up. If he plays you, just pass it. If one defender is back, it must be a layup. I don't want a jump shot on a 2-on-1 situation. Now, we have done 3/0, 3/2, and 2/1.

DIAGRAM 12-6.

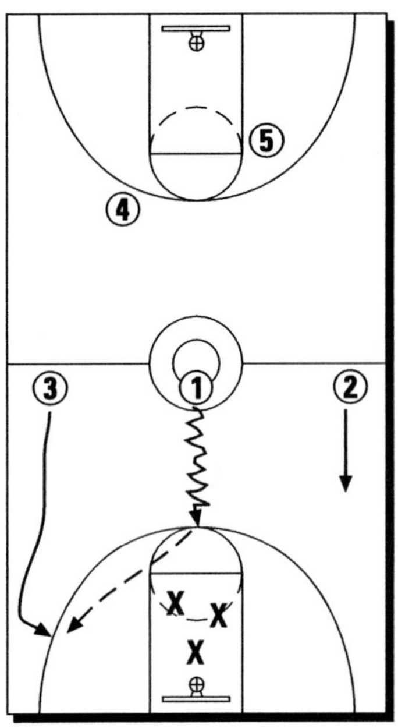

Before I get to Drill #4, I want to show you the secondary break and the drill that we use to work on it. Remember, if there are two or less defenders we want the primary break. But, let's say they have three defensive players back. 4 is the trailer, and 5 is the rebounder. Everybody must recognize what is going on, especially 1. There are three defenders. We want to flatten out the defense by taking the ball to the baseline. 1 dribbles off-center or passes to 3. Remember the rule, if he passes the ball, he follows his pass. If 1 passes to 3, he moves to the elbow on 3's side. The first big man down goes to the block, ballside, in this case, 4. The last big man down goes to the top of the key. The weakside wing goes to the foul line extended.

DIAGRAM 12-7.

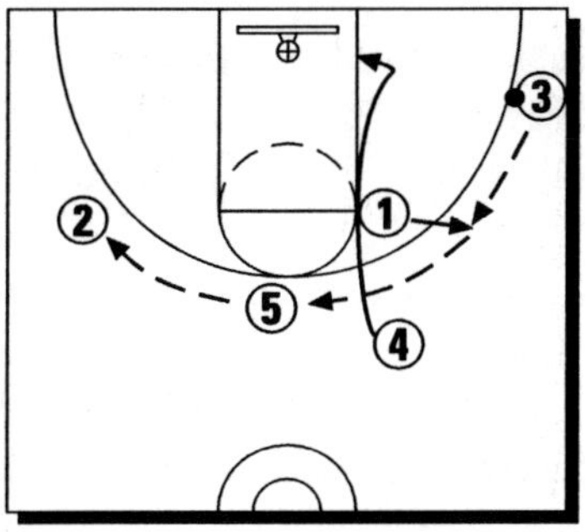

The first look of 3 who has the ball is inside. If it goes into 4, 4 and 5 are buddies. Anytime your buddy gets the ball, you go to the basket. So, 5 cuts to the basket. If 3 can't pass to 4, he passes to 1 who then looks into 4. Again, if 4 is not open, 3 passes to 5 who looks into 4. In the old days at North Carolina, we would run 3 off of 4, similar to a *flex cut,* because we had big players in these positions, and they were good shooters.

DIAGRAM 12-8.

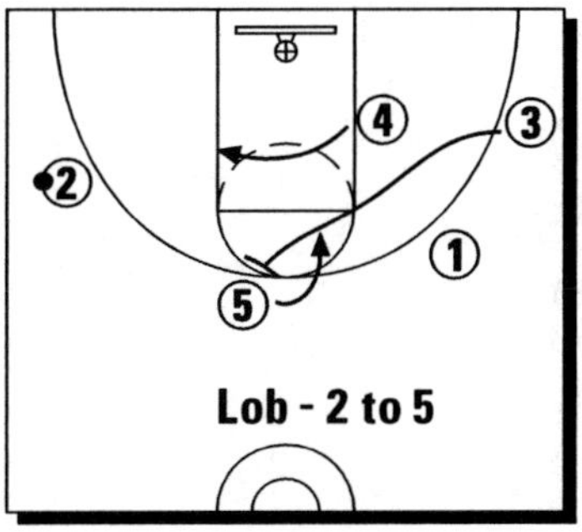

But, we changed it. We sent 4 across, and used 3 to set a rearscreen for 5 who cut to the basket looking for the lob. When the ball gets to 2, 4 has chased around following the ball. When the ball hits 5's hands, 3 moves to the block. When the ball is passed to 2, 3 makes the *rearscreen* for 5. 4 doesn't get it because he is fronted. 3's man ends up defending 5, and you should be able to get it to 5.

DIAGRAM 12-9.

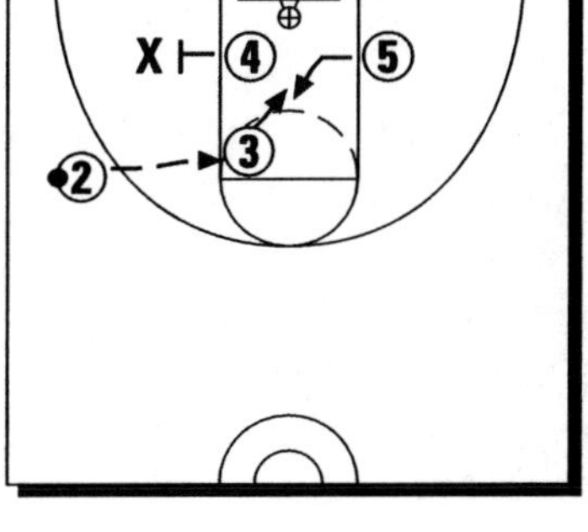

4 is now fronted; 5 is on the low block. If you can't get it to 5, you should be able to get it to 3. Then, 5 makes the duck-in move, and 4 seals.

DIAGRAM 12-10.

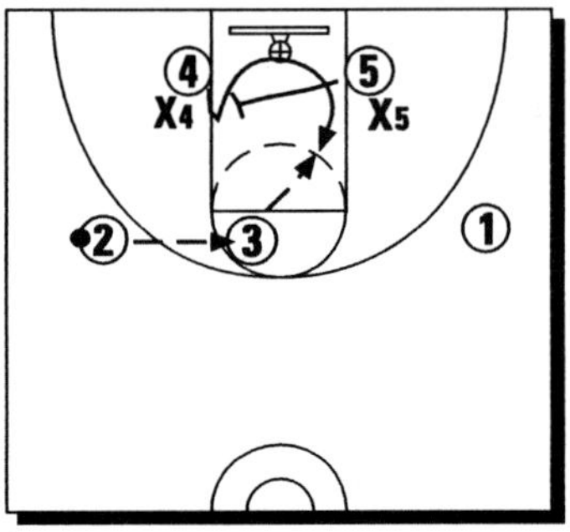

We have added something else. When 3 sets the screen, we want him to turn to the ball. We don't want him out high. We want to get him the ball at the foul line if we can. If 5 doesn't get the ball on the lob, he continues across and screens for 4. 4 must go baseline side. He must do this to allow room for 3 to operate. But also, 4 must look for anyone in that area to box him out. 5 has screened, and will then seal on the other side. So, we hope that there are no defenders between 4 and 5. Now, 3 must get them the ball or take one hard dribble and shoot because we have two inside positions on the board. That's our secondary break.

DIAGRAM 12-11. FAST BREAK DRILL #4—THE SECONDARY BREAK

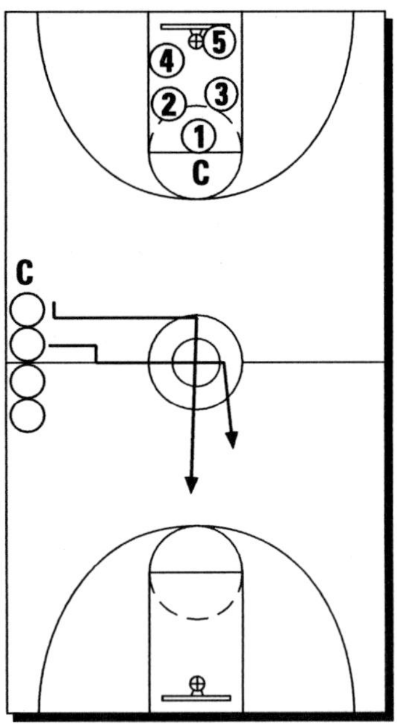

Initially, there are five players on the floor with no defense. There are five players off on the side near midcourt. These players each have a number. The coach there will call numbers, for example, 1 and 4, 3, all of you etc. The coach shoots, all five rebound. They then start to run the break to the other end. When the coach at midcourt says "go," the players called touch the center circle and get back on defense. It could be 5/3 or 5/1 or 5/5.

This is our *recognition drill.* As soon as we start down the court, we must recognize how many defenders will be in the play. If there are two or less defenders, we will have a shot with two or less passes. If there are more than two defenders, we will go into the *secondary break.* This year, four times in a two-game stretch, our opponent scored against us and, by the clock, four seconds later, we layed it up on the other end. That's demoralizing. So, we bust out and recognize the situation. If we have the *primary,* we pitch it ahead. If we don't, we go into the *secondary break.*

DIAGRAM 12-12. FAST BREAK DRILL #5

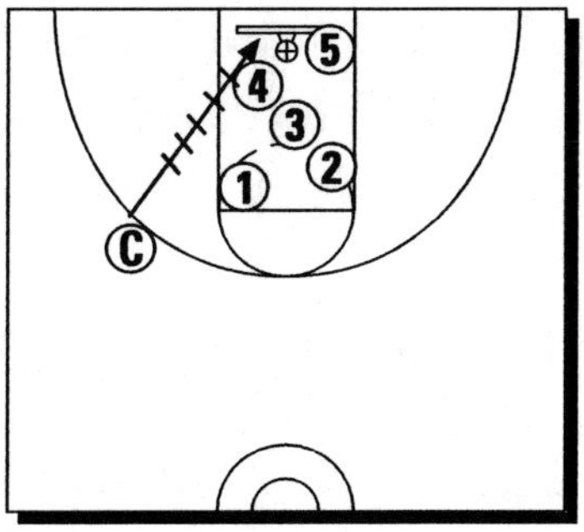

It's just 5/0; more than anything it is a conditioner. The coach shoots, and the ball may not touch the floor. There is no dribbling, no walking. You will hear the players talking. I've got the rebound, I've got the outlet. All five players must get to the top of the key extended. The drill is run in both directions. On a normal day, I want six layups — three on each end. We have two teams, the blue and the red. It is 5/0. I believe in having communication on offense. This drill helps. We do not use any other fast break drills for this purpose.

DIAGRAM 12-13.

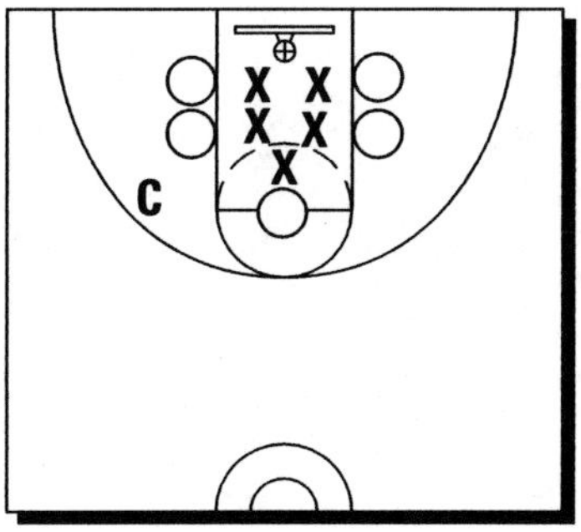

The only other thing we will do is play the *secondary break game.* We have 5/5. Coach shoots. If the defense gets the rebound, they break to the other end. If they make the *primary break,* that's fine. But now, I'm ticked off at the other team. If they make it, the other team jumps out of bounds and takes it the other way. We run the break after a made basket just like after a miss. We work on getting the ball out of the net quickly.

That is a good press offense. We do not assign 2 and 3 to a particular side. We want them to get down to the other end as fast as they can. It's like Abe Lemons said, "Coaching track must be the easiest sport to coach. Just stay to the left and get back as fast as you can." If 4 or 5 can get to the lane before 2 or 3, they run it. We believe in the *whole, part, and whole method.*

We start with the secondary break the first day of practice. Then, we break it down and do fast break drills #1 through #5. In our first two weeks of practice, we only do three things. We work on building our break, our halfcourt man-to-man defense, and our motion offense. If it's not one of those three areas, we don't work on it. This is our bread and butter. When a shot goes up, no matter what we are working on, we must change ends of the floor. If that team doesn't score, we must change ends again. If that team scores, we must sprint back, and then we stop it. We change ends twice on every 5/5 drill we use. *Primary break* is our first choice, *secondary break* is our second choice, and then *motion.* We want to attack you before you get set up.

THE PRESS OFFENSE

We basically have three positions for this, so I will label them 1, 2/3, and 4/5. This means that 2 and 3 are interchangeable, and so are 4 and 5. On every offensive set we have, 4 and 5 do the same thing, as do 2 and 3.

DIAGRAM 12-14.

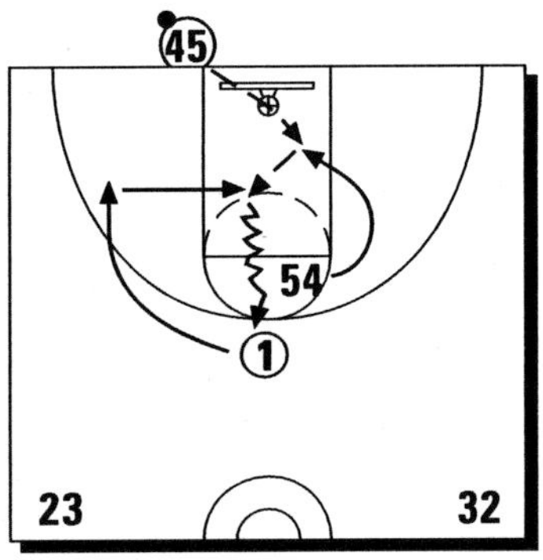

We have 4 or 5 take the ball out of the net and get it in to 1 immediately. 2 and 3 are at halfcourt. If 4 takes it in, 5 is near the elbow as the secondary outlet. Our first option is to get the ball directly to 1. We will run the press offense directly into the secondary break. If 1 can't get the ball, that means he is fronted. 5 will break to the ball. When 5 gets the pass, 1 will be open by breaking as shown.

DIAGRAM 12-15.

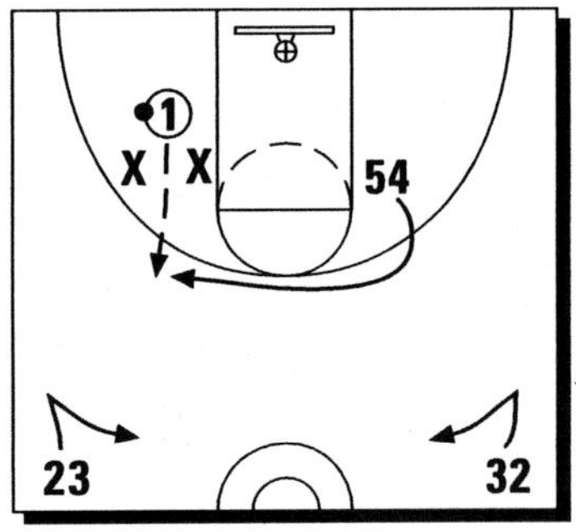

If 1 is doubleteamed, 5 will loop to the ball. Both 2 and 3 will loop back. This situation is easier for us because we can recruit a person who can beat the doubleteam.